THE
AUTISM INCLUSION & ACCESSIBILITY
BEGINNERS HANDBOOK

A GUIDE FOR ALLIES: FOSTERING INCLUSION IN THE COMMUNITY

BY

sunny
spectrum supports

SUNNY SPECTRUM SUPPORTS

ACKNOWLEDGEMENT OF COUNTRY

Sunny Spectrum Supports acknowledges and pays respect to the Kaurna people, the traditional custodians of the land on which our organisation operates. We pay respect to Elders past and present. We respect their spiritual beliefs and connections to land which are of ongoing importance to the living Kaurna people of today.

WITH THANKS

Sunny Spectrum Supports thanks the following collaborators for their contributions:

Project Team: Tamsin Dancer, Jasmine Deakin, Evan Johnson, Kendra McCann, Tammie Sinclair.

Autistic Advisory Group Members: Kate Donohue, Esther Fidock, Max Gow, Bec Jessop, Kate Pressler and Bec Secombe.

Special Thanks: Dr Emma Goodall, Marshall Buckley-Middleton and Susan Williams.

The development of this resource was funded by the South Australian Department for Education. All views and opinions expressed are that of Sunny Spectrum Supports Pty Ltd.

First published by Tamcan Pty Ltd in 2024
35 Ann Street, Salisbury SA 5108
National Library of Australia Cataloguing-in-Publication entry:

Sunny Spectrum Supports, 2024

ISBN: 978-0-6454582-2-0
eISBN: 978-0-6454582-3-7

ABOUT SUNNY SPECTRUM

Sunny Spectrum Supports is an Autistic-led social enterprise staffed by neurodivergent professionals. Our mission is for our community to feel safe, supported, included and welcomed. We uphold our commitment to neurodiversity affirming practice, and we believe that genuine inclusion is achieved through universal design, which starts with community education.

DISCLAIMER

This handbook and associated course materials were written and developed in 2024 and are designed to educate everyday people about autism. By offering insights into the lived experiences of Autistic people, it aims to raise awareness of barriers and ways to address them. It dispels common myths about autism, outlines what inclusion can strive for, and explains how everyone can contribute to improving outcomes for Autistic people.

The primary objective is to empower the community with the knowledge and confidence to promote inclusion and accessibility within various settings. While the content does not specifically address practice strategies for formal support professionals (such as allied health practitioners) or carers, it serves as a foundation for further learning.

It is important to note that each Autistic individual is unique, and the information presented in this handbook is of a general nature. While some tips in this handbook may be specific to autism/neurodivergence, many convey a universal message of compassion that can benefit the broader community. In an environment where individuals may require more patience and understanding, these principles embody a neurodiversity-affirming approach akin to universal design, fostering inclusivity and support for all.

Should you be interested in additional learning opportunities, Sunny Spectrum offers consultations, training sessions, and workshops to facilitate ongoing education and awareness.

CONTENTS

CONTENTS

1

INTRODUCTION

ABOUT

This handbook is a supplement to Sunny Spectrum Supports **"Autism Inclusion and Accessibility"** course; intended for members of the community who interact with and support Autistic people. It aims to provide a foundational understanding of autism and neurodiversity affirming / inclusive practice. The content of this handbook aligns with the South Australian State Autism Strategy's objective of making South Australia an autism-friendly state.

The main topics in this handbook include:

AUTISM 101	ACCESSIBILITY
REGULATION	**CONNECTION**

Coming away from this course, learners will feel more confident to foster:

CONNECTION
- *Confidently engaging with Autistic individuals*
- *Breaking down myths, stigmas, biases, and fears*

PARTICIPATION
- *Knowing how to be considerate of various support needs to enable meaningful participation*

INCLUSION
- *Taking steps achieve meaningful inclusion*
- *Understanding how to optimise spaces and environments to create accessibility beyond a social understanding (i.e., inclusive shops and offices).*

The resources associated with this handbook include:

- *Online learning course (available for separate purchase at www.sunnyspectrum.com.au)*

- *Glossary of common terms*

- *"Regulate, Connect & Support Guide"*

This handbook contains expanded content, including references to link back to evidence and research. Lived-experience insights, anecdotes and discussion points are provided throughout, along with tips and links to recommended further readings.

Throughout this handbook, you will see the following coloured boxes and icons with:

Lived-experience insights & anecdotes

Tips to support inclusion

Recommended links to further information

With Autistic people at its very core, this learning material embodies a genuine commitment to amplifying the voices and experiences of the Autistic community.

Participants stand to benefit from first-hand accounts, practical strategies, and nuanced insights from authors and facilitators who have first-hand lived-experience of being Autistic. Kind curiosity and meaningful conversation is encouraged.

Why does it matter?

Life outcomes for Autistic Australians are unacceptably poor.

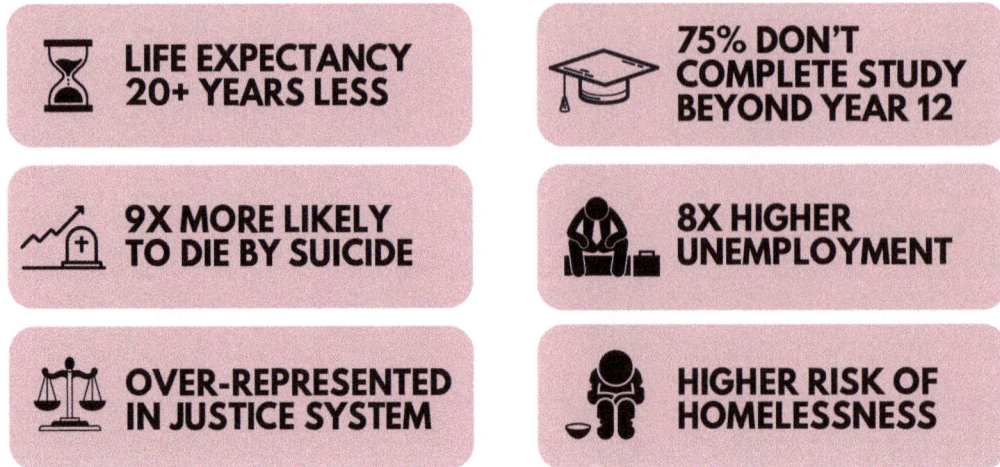

LIFE EXPECTANCY 20+ YEARS LESS	**75% DON'T COMPLETE STUDY BEYOND YEAR 12**
9X MORE LIKELY TO DIE BY SUICIDE	**8X HIGHER UNEMPLOYMENT**
OVER-REPRESENTED IN JUSTICE SYSTEM	**HIGHER RISK OF HOMELESSNESS**

This data is more than just words on a page; it represents the lived experiences of countless Autistic individuals who have been systematically denied opportunities to engage in activities that hold meaning and purpose for them, and to be safely included in society.

By highlighting this data and unpacking some of the common barriers faced by Autistic people, we can foster a deeper understanding, and work to achieve inclusive support approaches across critical life domains.

Despite the prevalence of autism, drivers of these poor outcomes are complex and interrelated with no single cause at the centre. Some examples include:

- *poor understanding within the community and among service providers*

- *a complex and poorly integrated service system*

- *unaccommodating environments*

- *workplace barriers*

- *delays in diagnosis and access to services*

- *exclusion and discrimination in generic disability services that are not designed to meet Autistic needs*

It is also acknowledged that intersectional identities result in some people being impacted disproportionally, including:

- *First Nations peoples*

- *People from lower socio-economic backgrounds*

- *LGBTQIA+ people*

- *People from culturally and linguistically diverse backgrounds*

- *People in regional and remote locations*

- *People in the child protection and criminal justice systems*

- *People with multiple and complex needs*

Greater understanding of autism can help dispel misconceptions, reduce stigma, and stop the spread of misinformation as we move towards a more inclusive and equitable society.

THE EXACT NUMBER OF AUTISTIC PEOPLE IS UNKNOWN, BUT IT IS QUITE LIKELY THAT YOU FREQUENTLY ENGAGE WITH MEMBERS OF THE AUTISTIC COMMUNITY.

Due to inconsistent data it isn't known exactly how many people are Autistic. Some data suggests that it could be 1 in 70 people, more recent data suggests that it is 1 in 36 children. Given that children grow into adults, it would make sense that 1 in 36 adults are Autistic.

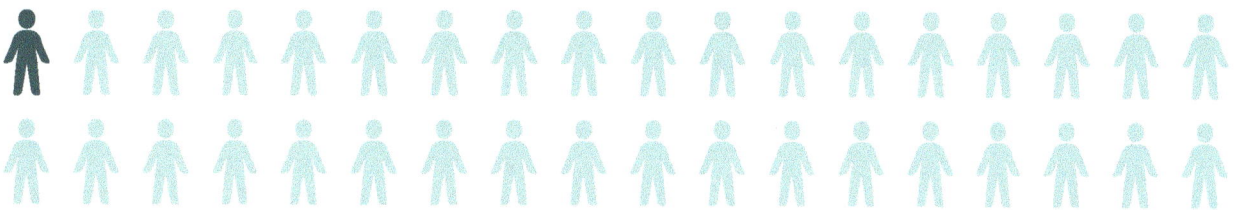

It is probable that 1 in 36 people is a more accurate statistic. Inconsistent data could be due to a range of factors including: inaccessibility of diagnostic assessment, lack of information, fears of stigma, gender and cultural bias in diagnostic tools, gaps in clinical knowledge (i.e. the autism "assessor" lacks knowledge about different ways a person may present) and/or previous misdiagnosis.

LANGUAGE

Throughout this handbook and associated learning materials, identity-first language is used due to this being the preference of a large proportion of the Autistic community. It is recognised that language preferences around identity are a personal decision, and some Autistic people may identify otherwise.

"OUR IDENTITIES MAKE US WHO WE ARE, AND ALL ASPECTS OF OUR IDENTITIES ARE IMPORTANT, INCLUDING (MAYBE EVEN SPECIFICALLY) OUR DISABILITIES."

— *CHLOÉ HAYDEN*

Examples of widely adopted language preferences that we use include:

We don't say ✗	Instead, we say ✓
Person with / has autism	Autistic person
Suffers from autism	Autistic person
Lives with autism	Autistic person
Autism Spectrum Disorder (ASD)	Autism

It is appreciated when non-Autistic people model community language preferences.

Sunny Spectrum Supports Regulate, Connect & Support Guide.

2

AUTISM 101

What is autism & neurodiversity?

WHAT IS AUTISM?

"WE NEED TO UNDERSTAND AUTISTIC PEOPLE BETTER, NOT TRY TO CHANGE WHO THEY ARE."

-CHRIS PACKHAM

In 2024, the South Australian Government implemented a State Autism Strategy. Extensive community engagement determined that the favoured definition of autism in South Australia is:

"Autism is a neurological developmental difference that impacts the way an Autistic person sees, experiences, understands and responds to the world. Every person's lived experience of autism is different"

In other words, autism is a brain difference; thinking, feeling and existing in a way that is different to, and diverges away from, the majority of people. For the majority, autism is an important part of who they are and how they experience the world around them.

Autistic brains grow and develop differently to non-Autistic brains, and this is usually considered to be genetically "hard-wired" from birth.

Emerging research indicates that **autism should not be viewed as a problem that needs to be fixed**, as doing so can have detrimental effects on an Autistic persons life outcomes.

Many non-Autistic people think that being "labelled" Autistic doesn't define who someone is, however many *Autistic* people describe autism as an inherent part of who they are that forms part of their identity.

There is evidence to suggest that identifying as Autistic contributes to positive wellbeing. **Simply, knowing who we are, and why, is a good thing!**

Some things that Autistic people might do differently include:

COMMUNICATING AND NAVIGATING THE WORLD

THINKING AND PROCESSING INFORMATION

COORDINATING BODIES AND MOVEMENT

REGULATING THE BODY AND MIND

This may include some/all of the following:

- *Passionate interests*

- *Differences with using eye contact or having fluctuating eye contact*

- *Use of direct communication*

- *Differences in interpreting body language and facial expressions*

- *Differing social preferences*

- *Echolalia (repeating words or phrases)*

- *Preference for eating "same foods"*

- *Sensory processing differences*

- *Stimming (self-stimulatory behaviours)*

- *Preference for routine, predictability and structure*

- *Great attention to detail, "bottom up thinking"*

- *The use of alternative communication*

- *Preference for literal language, thinking in "black and white"*

- *Monotropic focus ("tunnel vision")*

Never assume that all Autistic people have the exact same experiences or presentations.

SUPPORT NEEDS

When a person receives an autism diagnosis, they are assigned a "level" of either 1, 2 or 3. These levels are determined by of the amount of support that an individual requires based on their "functioning" at the time of assessment. The assignment of a level is part of the autism diagnostic process, however, it doesn't always capture the reality of a person's support needs.

Many members of the Autistic community prefer not to use terms like "high functioning" or "low functioning", as they inaccurately describe the levels of 'severity', or the level of difficulty that an individual faces (although, some people still prefer these terms to describe their experience).

> Many Autistic self-advocates reject the use of "functioning labels" as every person's degree of functioning fluctuates day to day, within contexts, and across different domains of life.
>
> **Ask yourself:** Do you function the same every day?

A linear spectrum does not consider Autistic individual differences or fluctuating needs. "High functioning" often minimises support needs, and "low functioning" often minimises abilities and opportunities. The linear spectrum may also give rise to assumptions about someone's capabilities without actually knowing the individual.

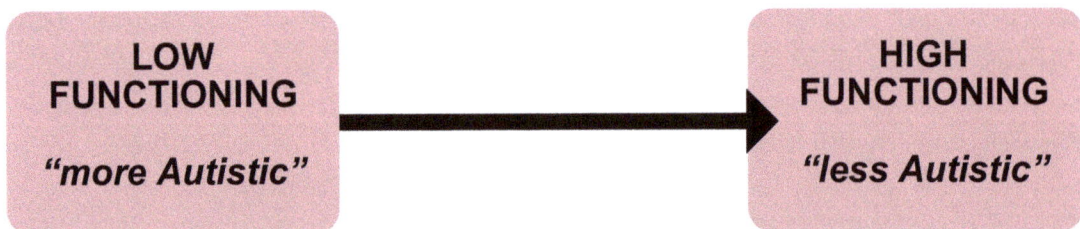

LOW FUNCTIONING *"more Autistic"*	→	HIGH FUNCTIONING *"less Autistic"*

This approach can be problematic because it can suggest that the Autism Spectrum is linear, i.e., goes from less Autistic to more Autistic, and perpetuates unhelpful stereotypes.

https://Autisticadvocacy.org/2021/12/functioning-labels-harm-Autistic-people/

Consider these examples of stereotypes...

Low Functioning:
Assumed intellectual disability and generally receives, more support and services.

Challenges may include:
Infantilisation, significantly less representation, often don't get a voice in community, less education and employment choices and opportunities.

High Functioning:
Assumed to have a high "IQ" and generally receives little to no support.

Challenges may include:
Demands often outweigh capacity, little recognition of challenges and are usually expected to participate in education and employment without support.

It serves no helpful purpose to refer to an Autistic person as either "high functioning", "low functioning", *or* level 1, 2 or 3 in everyday conversation *(noting that this terminology is still used in the medical world, which is discussed on the next page).*

A more neuro-affirming approach would include discussing support needs in different aspects of life, acknowledging that they are unique to the individual and often fluctuate.

We can instead talk about **low, medium**, and **high** support needs.

However, it is important to note that a person can have differing support needs across different life domains, for example, low communication support needs and high sensory support needs; or they may have similar needs across areas.

Someone's support needs can also be increased by neurotypical expectations in different environments. For example, in order to perform the same as neurotypical people at school or in the workplace an individual might need additional support and accommodations.

Society was not designed with Autistic people in mind. A capitalist society values people for how productive they are in a typical work context. This can lead Autistic people to masking *(further discussed on page 45)* as well as internalised ableism, lack of self-esteem, or outright exclusion. Autistic people often have different skill sets and may need accommodations and support to thrive in a neurotypical world.

Put simply, Autistic support needs refer to the amount of support an individual requires to complete daily living tasks and activities.

These needs are not determined by how outwardly Autistic someone appears, nor by the timing of their assessment or how they presented on their assessment day.

"Support needs" differ from functioning labels or "levels" of autism, as they recognise the range and diversity of supports each individual may require.

This approach to Autistic functioning can be visualised a little more like this:

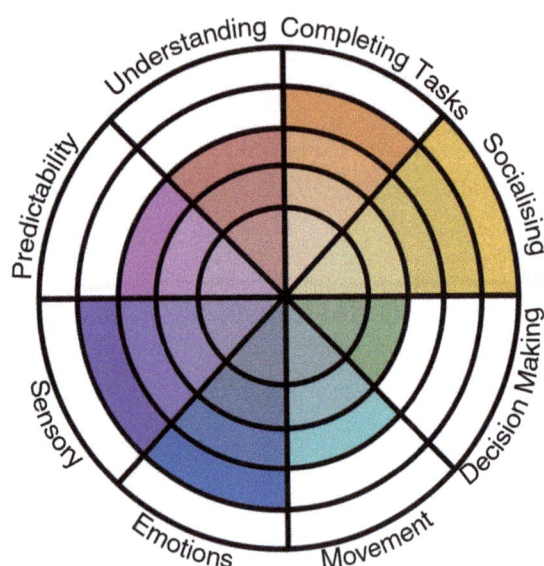

Consider the different colour shades/gradients as indicators of the amount of support needed in each area: fewer filled boxes indicate less support is required, while more filled boxes indicate a greater need for support.

This support wheel, and similar wheels, can represent varying needs across different areas of life, making it easier to understand a person and their varied support needs. It also highlights 'spiky profiles' where individuals might have lower support needs in some areas and higher needs in others.

https://enna.org/why-the-Autistic-community-are-rejecting-the-terms-high-and-low-functioning/

It is best to ask someone about support needs rather than relying on labels. Support needs can often vary day to day, sometimes even minute to minute, so you might need to ask more on more than one occasion or in different settings.

Examples of varied and fluctuating support needs:

Danny may find they can focus on studying at home in a quiet environment, however, they struggle at school and find it overwhelming. Therefore, their support needs for studying at school will be different, such as having access to noise-cancelling headphones. **This is an example of fluctuating support needs for sensory experiences.**

Alice's tolerance for nervous system dysregulation and overwhelm may fluctuate day to day, impacting her ability to process information and think clearly. Sometimes she can be completely independent in participating in her necessary tasks, while other times she may need significant support. **This is an example of fluctuating support needs for sensory and/or social experiences and completing daily living tasks**

Lauren is non-speaking and uses Augmentative and Alternative Communication (AAC) in all contexts. She finds most environments over-stimulating and will self-soothe to feel calmer, however, she still has frequent meltdowns. She needs support in completing all of her self-care tasks and lives in a supported living arrangement. **This is an example of consistently high support needs for communication, sensory regulation and daily living tasks.**

Jacob is independent in all of his activities of daily living, but uses reminder systems in case he forgets things. He sometimes find social cues confusing making social interactions tricky. He can be overwhelmed by noise but can self-manage this with noise cancelling headphones. **This is an example of low to medium support needs for sensory experiences, communication and daily living tasks that can be managed independently.**

NEURODIVERSITY

All humans think and experience the world in different ways; this is called neurodiversity. The word neurodiversity describes the overarching concept that there is no one "right" way for people to think, learn, and behave.

The term "neurodiverse" refers to a *group* with diversity among ways of thinking.

Consider the concept of biodiversity; plants, animals, fungi, all co-existing. The same applies to neurodiversity; all different brain types and perspectives coexisting. Just as a tree cannot be "biodiverse" on its own, a singular person is not neurodiverse, but they are a *part* of neurodiversity.

In the following example, each shape represents different ways of thinking and being (different "neurotypes"):

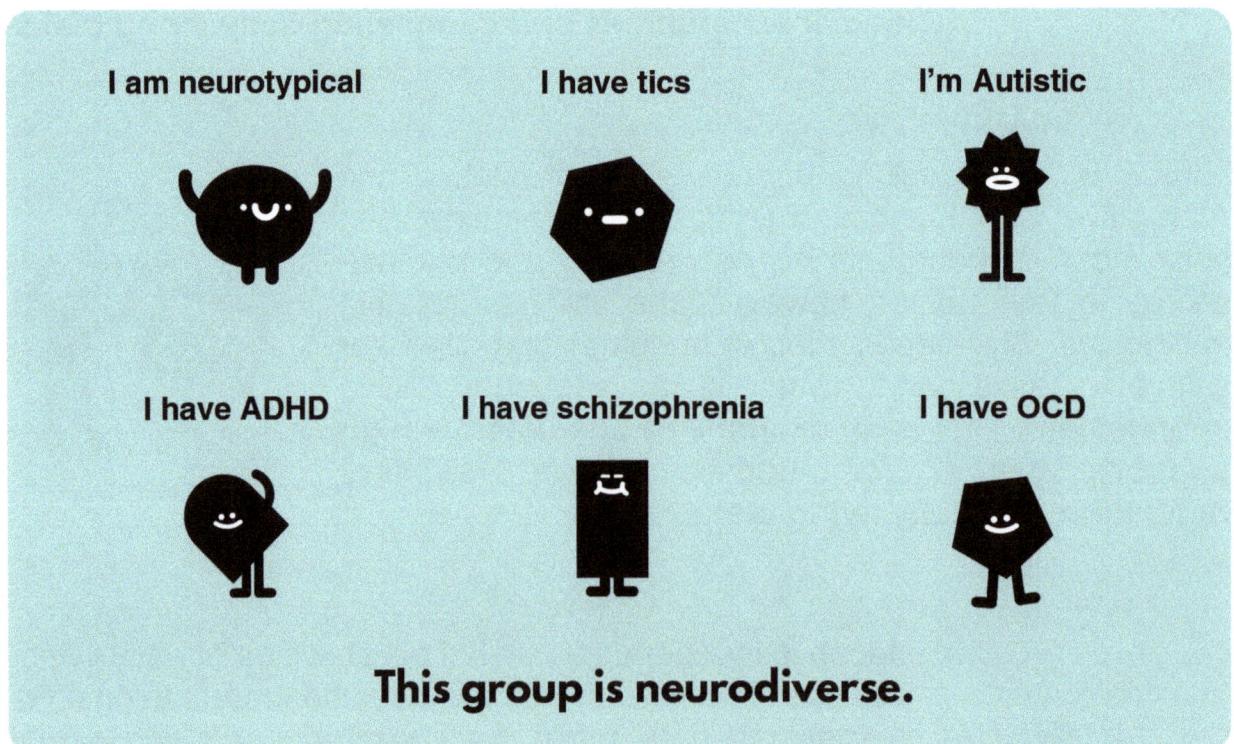

I am neurotypical	I have tics	I'm Autistic

I have ADHD	I have schizophrenia	I have OCD

This group is neurodiverse.

WE CAN THINK ABOUT NEURODIVERSITY AS THE NATURAL VARIABILITY OF COGNITIVE AND FUNCTIONAL ABILITIES IN <u>ALL PEOPLE</u>.

What about "Neurodivergent?"

The terms "*neurodiverse*" and "*neurodivergent*" *have different meanings.*

The term neurodivergent refers to a person who diverges from the "typical" or the most common neurotype. It is an "umbrella" term that encompasses the many ways in which a brain can operate *differently* to the majority of people.

Let's take a look at a different group of shapes....

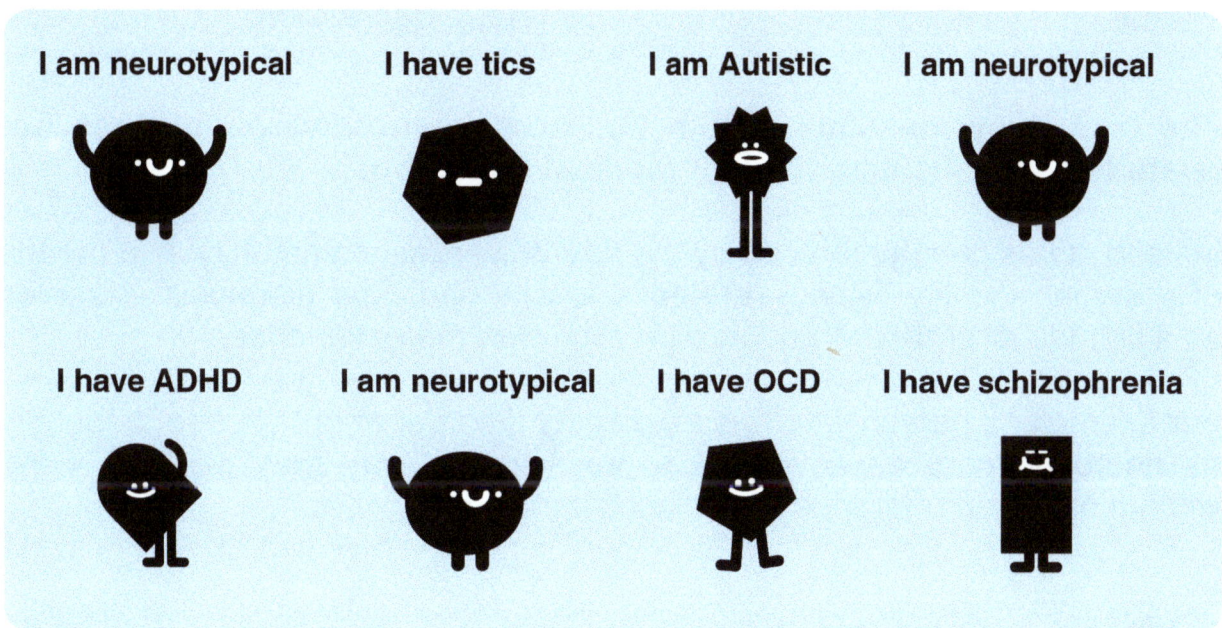

I am neurotypical	I have tics	I am Autistic	I am neurotypical

I have ADHD	I am neurotypical	I have OCD	I have schizophrenia

This group is still neurodiverse, as there are a range of different neurotypes. However, we can see that 😈 is the most common and, therefore, the dominant neurotype.

The following shapes <u>diverge</u> from the dominant neurotype, therefore, they are neuro<u>divergent</u>.

I have ADHD	I have tics	I am Autistic	I have OCD	I have schizophrenia

Neurodivergent people may have different strengths and challenges because of their differences.

Differences may be:

- *genetic and neurodevelopmental (e.g. autism, ADHD)*

- *acquired (e.g. brain injury)*

- *medical condition (e.g. epilepsy)*

- *learning disabilities (e.g. dyslexia)*

- *intellectual disability*

- *mental health related (e.g. depression)*

The take away message is that the word "neurodivergent" does not relate to a <u>specific</u> diagnosis or medical condition.

Instead, it has been embraced by the neurodivergent community as a means of asserting identity without reference to any particular diagnosis. It serves as a self-identifier for individuals who align with the experience.

For example, a person who has an anxiety disorder might choose to identify as neurodivergent as a way of expressing the way they see the world without having to reference a medical diagnosis.

Much like how many people *identify* as either an introvert or extrovert - One cannot be *diagnosed* as an introvert or extrovert; rather, individuals identify with the term. It is same with the word "neurodivergent".

If someone tells you that they are neurodivergent, it is not relevant or appropriate to ask them about their diagnosis *(unless you have a reason to know, such as being a formal support person);* but keep in mind "neurodivergent" doesn't always mean Autistic.

Avoid language such as "neurodivergent condition". This is because these two words oppose each other (neurodivergent= identity; condition= medical diagnosis).

THE "MOVEMENT"

Autism is diagnosed with the DSM-5-TR (often referred to as the "DSM" for short), a diagnostic manual for mental disorders. The DSM lists series of deficits (i.e., problems) and a person is diagnosed if they have those deficits. This approach is aligned with the "medical model" of disability.

The medical model of disability states that an individual is in need of being "fixed" or "cured". The emphasis is on the individual and faults them for their disability. It focuses on what the person cannot do and cannot be.

MEDICAL MODEL

"What is wrong with the person? How do we fix them?"

Instead, the social model of disability sees the interaction between the individual and their physical, social, institutional, and attitudinal environments. It implies that the environmental factors are what is disabling and must change for individuals to participate. It does not blame the individual for their disability. It does not deny the reality of impairment nor impact on the individual, instead, it challenges environmental factors to accommodate natural human diversity.

SOCIAL MODEL

"What support does this person need?"

HUMAN RIGHTS MODEL

"How can we ensure this person has the same rights as everyone else?

The neurodiversity movement is a human rights movement towards acceptance of all neurotypes, and the acknowledgement that no person is deficient or flawed because of the way their brain is wired. It is a move towards dismantling the barriers imposed by society to accessing required supports and conditions for all brain types to thrive.

> Our society is caught somewhere between the medical, social and human rights model of disability. For example, "proving" disability requires the use of medical i.e., deficit based assessments, despite the fact that we know that the social and human rights models are best-practice.

AUTISM IS AN INTERNAL AND EXTERNAL EXPERIENCE

Understanding autism requires a nuanced perspective that goes beyond medical diagnostic criteria. It involves appreciating the intricate relationship between an individual's internal experiences and the external environment. This holistic view acknowledges that autism is not solely a personal journey but one deeply influenced by societal contexts and interactions.

By exploring both the internal aspects, such as sensory processing and cognitive differences, and external factors such as societal attitudes and accessibility, we can better grasp the full scope of how autism is shaped by the world around us.

This dual perspective highlights the importance of considering both hidden disabilities (internal) and the social model of disability (external) to include and support Autistic people to meaningfully participate in all aspects of life.

WHEN WE THINK OF AUTISM AS AN INTERNAL AND EXTERNAL EXPERIENCE, WE RECOGNISE THE DYNAMIC RELATIONSHIP BETWEEN AN INDIVIDUAL AND THEIR ENVIRONMENT.

The upcoming segments of this handbook will delve deeper into both the internal and external aspects of autism.

HIDDEN DISABILITY

When you think about Autism, what comes to mind?

You may think of stereotypes you've seen depicted in media of how an Autistic person looks and behaves. However, stereotypes are just that – generalisations that may or may not be true about an Autistic person. If you've met one Autistic person…you've met *one* Autistic person, every individual has unique needs and differences.

Autism is often referred to as a "hidden disability", and someone may have a wide variety of support needs that are unmet because they remain unnoticed.

Autism is a hidden mosaic of individuality, not a certain "look".

Yet, whilst appearing like everyone else, we are navigating a world designed without us in mind which can be disabling.

Have you heard of the hidden disabilities sunflower?

The Hidden Disabilities Sunflower is a symbol worn voluntarily by many people to self-disclose a disability or condition that may not be immediately apparent. This symbol communicates the potential need for assistance, understanding, or additional time in various settings such as shops, workplaces, public transport, or other public spaces. Typically, the most recognisable identifier is a green lanyard with yellow sunflowers worn around the neck, although some may opt for a sunflower badge or other wearable item.

https://hdsunflower.com/au/

It's important to note that not all people with hidden disabilities choose to wear a sunflower symbol, so it's important to keep this in mind when interacting with non-outwardly disclosing individuals.

We all have different experiences...

While it is true that many Autistic people align with the idea of having a hidden disability, some Autistic people describe their experiences as not being invisible or hidden at all!

With an increased focus on autism awareness, discussions have largely centred around hidden signs of autism and late diagnosis. Whilst this has enabled access to valuable information, this narrative fails to capture the diverse range of experiences within the Autistic community. For example, some individuals may conceal their Autistic traits in familiar surroundings but may struggle with adapting to new environments, causing their Autistic traits to seem more apparent. Some may have never learned or wanted to hide their Autistic traits at all.

It's important to always be inclusive and accommodating from the beginning, no matter who you're engaging with, and to not judge someone based on what you are seeing in the moment. Empathy goes a long way in supporting Autistic people.

Remember that disability is dynamic, meaning it can look different for people in different situations.

"Whilst my disability is technically "hidden", there are times when some of my experiences such as anxiety or a meltdown are visible, and in stressful instances I may choose to wear my Sunflower lanyard or wrap it around the straps of my handbag." - **Autistic Adult**

How an Autistic person communicates, moves their body and interacts with the world and/or variations in support needs often mean that there are also variations in how "visible" a persons disability is.

sunny
spectrum supports

3

REGULATION

Internal: On the inside

INTERNAL EXPERIENCES
The Nervous System

The nervous system is like the body's communication network. It's responsible for sending messages between different parts of your body and your brain. The nervous system is always working behind the scenes to keep your body and mind safe and running smoothly. Think of it as a network of roads that connects different parts of the body to the brain. Just as roads allow cars to travel from one place to another, the nervous system sends messages throughout the body.

"Nervous system regulation" refers to how the brain manages and controls these messages, similar to a traffic cop directing the flow of information.

An important part of the cops' job is to continually run background scans for signs of safety, danger or life-threat. It checks messages from inside the body *(energy, pain or illness)* and from the outside *(others' actions, non-verbal communications, sounds, smells)* very quickly and **outside of our awareness**.

You might be familiar with the "fight, flight, freeze" response. There are more responses that are recognised as part of this response, including "fawn" *(giving in to the threat)* and "flop" *(shut-down)*.

These are primitive human responses that prepare the body to handle acute stressors, for example, increasing heart rate and alertness so that you can run away from danger.

THE PROBLEM IS...OUR BRAINS CAN REACT THE SAME WHETHER WE ARE BEING CHASED BY A BEAR OR WE ARE ANXIOUS FOR SOME OTHER REASON.

Kids Helpline Fight Flight Freeze explanation
https://www.youtube.com/watch?v=HDFIuNzX19w

What this means is...

At times, our bodies and brains may perceive a situation as life-threatening, triggering a response that prepares us for immediate action, even if the threat is relatively minor.

Even minor threats can cause an imbalance in the primary parts of the nervous system, leading to one part working harder than the other. This state is referred to as "dysregulation".

A DYSREGULATED NERVOUS SYSTEM AFFECTS EMOTIONAL AND PHYSICAL WELLBEING.

External environmental factors are known to create anxiety and stress in Autistic people, leading to heightened nervous system activity.

A number of stressful factors are known to contribute to dysregulation, including:

STIGMA. BULLYING, EXCLUSION

Leading to feeling unsafe, low levels of self-compassion and social isolation

SENSORY OVERSTIMULATION

As a result of sensory processing differences and 'unfriendly' environments

COGNITIVE OVERLOAD

Often occurs when expected to conform to 'neurotypical' standards

💡 Dysregulation isn't always visible on the outside, though, it may present in behaviour and how someone functions *(e.g. memory)*. Some dysregulated people may also not notice how or what is dysregulating them, requiring them to stop and assess the signs unique to them.

📖 Dr Dan Siegel's Hand Model of the Brain: https://www.youtube.com/watch?v=f-m2YcdMdFw&t=333s

All of these influences can create stress in the nervous system and send a message that the world is unsafe. When this occurs too much or for too long, the nervous system enters a state of overwhelm.

Overwhelm could look like:

MELTDOWN   **SHUTDOWN**   **BURNOUT**

We will take a look at each of these experiences in more depth on page 45.

It is important to understand that when such experiences happen, the nervous system is not failing and the individual is not faulty. The nervous system is designed to provide protection and adapt to its environment. In an environment not adapted to the needs of the Autistic individual, such reactions are protective. It is helpful to remember this as it counters self-blame / shame and promotes acceptance and compassion.

IF STRESS AND ANXIETY IS REDUCED, AUTISTIC NERVOUS SYSTEM FUNCTIONING IMPROVES!

> You can have a role to play in creating environments that reduce stress and anxiety; as a key driver of overwhelm often includes sensory and social aspects of the environment.

> If you notice that someone may be dysregulated, connecting through compassion and empathy can help. When people receive compassion, they find it easier to be compassionate toward themselves.
>
> **Compassion and self-compassion are associated with a calm nervous system.**

As humans, our nervous systems are designed to tune into each other. This means that when one person is "dysregulated" it can affect the other person. The good news is that the reverse is also true; **when one person is calm, it can help another person to feel calm.** This is known as emotional contagion and it can happen automatically just by being present with someone.

> When people have not had many safe experiences it can take them a long time to trust, but showing up consistently as a non-judgemental safe person can help build capacity to benefit from co-regulation.

Connection to self, others and the environment around you is vital for the human experience. Understanding who you are, your values and your purpose is important to everyone, Autistic or not. Knowing what you love and enjoy will allow the connection to self and also the connection to others and the world around you.

Human connection enriches life, fostering empathy, understanding, and emotional support. It brings about a sense of belonging, reducing the feeling of being lonely and isolated. Through interaction, people gain diverse perspective, fostering personal growth and resilience. Social connection supports overall health including mental well-being and promotes happiness. **Human connection nourishes wellbeing and fosters a sense of community.**

> One of the most effective ways to connect with an Autistic person is by engaging with what brings them joy. Even if their interests aren't your own, valuing and supporting these passions can be meaningful, as they can play a key role in wellbeing. **There's no need to become an expert on their interests - staying curious and open is what matters most.**

> You may have heard the term "body doubling" - this is a great strategy to aid co-regulation. It involves one person being alongside another while they complete a task that they would otherwise find challenging.

INTERNAL EXPERIENCES
The Sensory System

The sensory system is a network of nerves and receptors throughout the body that gather information from the environment and take messages back to the brain to be processed.

Each sensory system is responsible for gathering specific types of information: for example, the eyes (visual) detect light and colours, ears (auditory) detect sound waves, and skin (somatosensory) detects pressure, temperature, and texture.

When sensory information reaches the brain it is interpreted. How you process that information determines how you make sense of the world around you and navigate through daily life.

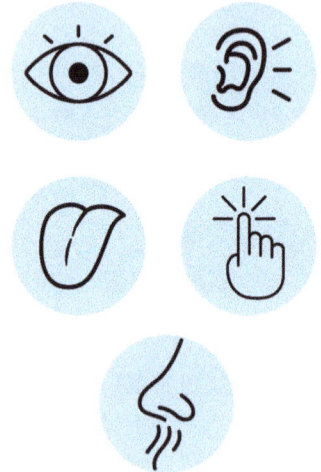

Most of us have heard of the body's five senses: sight, hearing, taste, touch, and smell.

There are other senses that are not as well-known...

Proprioception: How you perceive position and movement in space without having to look, enabling balance and coordination.

Vestibular: Detects changes in head position, movement and makes sense of gravity. It is responsible for balance and stability

Interoception: The perception of internal body signals. It helps you respond to certain body signals such as thirst, hunger, pain, when you need to toilet.

https://neurodivergentinsights.com/blog/8-senses

It has been suggested that up to 94% of Autistic adults have sensory reactivity differences.

This likely means that most Autistic people process sensory information differently to non-Autistic people.

These differences in processing can show up as:

Sensory hypersensitive (more sensitive):
Experiencing sensory input more strongly and can find it painful, dysregulating, or overwhelming.

Sensory hyposensitive (less sensitive):
May have delayed responses, or not even notice sensory input.

Sensory seeking (craving):
Deliberately engaging with sensory input more frequently and for sustained periods of time.

Sensory avoidance:
Deliberately engaging with sensory input less, moving away or blocking certain sensory input.

Using the example of sound, these could be explained as:

HYPERSENSITIVITY

Background music may be distracting or overstimulating when trying to listen to someone speaking.

HYPOSENSITIVITY

Music (even alarms) may not be noticed or easier to ignore, meaning an individual may need louder or different types of input to activate a response.

SENSORY SEEKING

Loud music may feel euphoric, which may mean an individual requires louder music to meet their sensory needs

Many **sensory profiles** are complex and someone may be sensitive to some inputs, may "seek out" different types of sensory input and miss some sensory cues all together! For example:

- Being more sensitive to loud shopping centres *(sound hypersensitivity)* but not respond when their name is called *(sound hyposensitivity)*
  OR
- Experiencing discomfort during a haircut and refusing to go *(touch hypersensitivity and sensory discomfort)* but getting enjoyment from tight hugs *(touch hyposensitivity and sensory seeking)*.

Understanding each individual's unique sensory profile would be an impossible task. However, it is essential not to generalise that all Autistic people have identical sensory experiences or require identical accommodations.

It is common to feel more hyperreactive/sensitive when already overwhelmed, meaning other stimuli *(like competing sounds, bright or flickering lights, light touch, clothing etc.)* can create a vicious cycle of hypersensitivity where distress amplifies the brain's hyper-vigilance, leading to even more distress.

Why this is highlighted...

Repeated exposure to distressing sensory experiences is linked to poor mental health outcomes such as anxiety, depression, and eating disorders, as well as **Autistic burnout** *(which is discussed further on page 46)*. It can even have poor physical health outcomes, such as hearing damage from seeking loud music, or a high pain tolerance leading to poor medical care.

By understanding the reasons behind sensory overwhelm and its impact on life outcomes, you can understand the importance of addressing sensory needs.

https://studentwellbeinghub.edu.au/educators/topics/interoception-and-self-regulation/

Autistic people report a range of helpful and unhelpful techniques to cope with their sensory differences:

Avoidance includes leaving the environment as well as blocking one's eyes, ears, nose, or holding breath.

Adaptations such as wearing sunglasses to cope with overhead lights, or earplugs/headphones to cope with shopping centres.

Soothing sensory input such as using a fidget or carrying a comfort item to hold when overwhelmed or "stimming".

Support and understanding from partners, family, and friends when trying to cope with sensory differences.

> Repeated exposure to distressing stimuli does not help build tolerance or resilience, it may do the opposite by creating further negative association.

Many Autistic people self-regulate their sensory system, or even communicate something, by "stimming". Some examples of stimming may include:

- *Repetitive movements*
- *Repetitive sounds*
- *Rocking*
- *Fidgeting*
- *Flapping*
- *Hair twirling*
- *Bouncing a leg*
- *Repeating a sound, word or phrase*

Sunny Spectrum Supports Glossary.

"It looks like they're stimming, are they OK?"

You might notice an Autistic person regulating their sensory system, by stimming, but this doesn't always mean they are in distress.

Autistic people use "stimming" for a range of reasons, such as:

Helping their mind focus on a task

Choosing to taking a break from being still (sensory break)

Communicating without words

Express joy and satisfaction

The autism diagnostic criteria recognises stimming (repetitive sounds and movements) as deficits (i.e., problems to fix). Considering what an effective coping mechanism stimming can be for self-regulation, why would we ever want to stop*?
*As long as it is safe.

If someone is engaging in unsafe stimming, for example head-banging, chewing on unsafe items, or another type of self-harm, you can help by:

- removing harmful items from the environment
- reducing any sensory factors leading to the distress
- telling a carer or consistent support person who is adequately trained to intervene

Autistic people often experience things deeply and intensely; happiness may feel like overwhelming joy, and frustration may feel like explosive rage. Stimming can occur with joy, not just distress!

MELTDOWNS

Autistic meltdowns are an involuntary response to an overwhelming situation where the individual temporarily loses control. Meltdowns can look different for every individual.

Often mistakenly thought of as temper tantrums, meltdowns occur when there is sensory and/or cognitive overload usually mixed with an expectation or demand that cannot be met.

Unlike a temper tantrum, the individual is not attempting to manipulate a situation and cannot easily switch it off. They are usually exhausting, can sometimes take days to recover from, and can also be followed by feelings of shame.

Understanding how an Autistic person may feel internally during a meltdown can help you to empathise and provide effective support.

There are 6 stages to a meltdown:

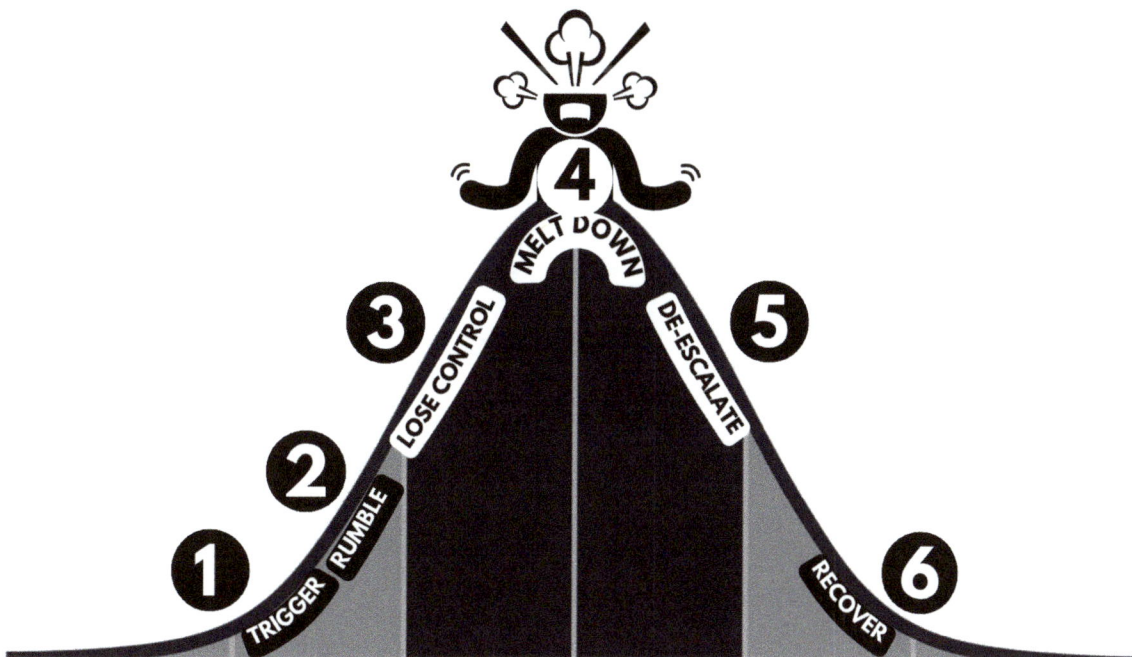

The Mighty: 15 People on the Autism Spectrum Describe What a Meltdown Feels Like: https://themighty.com/topic/autism-spectrum-disorder/what-autism-meltdowns-feel-like-for-Autistic-people/

What do the 6 stages of a meltdown look and feel like?

① Trigger Stage

A trigger is something that *happens* that sends the nervous system into survival mode. Usually a trigger involves a specific stimulus (such as a word, sound, smell, or situation). Some triggers might include:

- *feeling trapped*
- *change of routine*
- *demand overwhelm*
- *sensory overwhelm or under-stimulation*
- *can't regulate body temperature*
- *physical pain, illness or lack of sleep*
- *difficulty identifying/regulating emotions*

> **The trigger may not be the entire reason for the meltdown. Think of it as the "last straw".**

② Rumble Stage

After there has been a trigger that the body/brain has perceived as a threat, there will be signs of dysregulation/overwhelm that suggest a meltdown could be rumbling, such as:

- *difficulty with, or change in communication*
- *isolation or running away*
- *needing frequent reassurance*
- *experiencing sensory distress*
- *increase in stimming*
- *loss of focus /exhaustion*
- *losing ability to mask*
- *appearing flushed*

> **It may still possible to "come back down" and avoid a meltdown if we recognise the signs of "rumbling" and act calmly and quickly.**

❸ Losing Control Stage

If dysregulation / overwhelm is not resolved during the "rumble" stage, it is likely that the person will start to lose control and enter a meltdown.

> **There is usually no coming back once we have lost control. We simply need to "ride it out".**
>
> When we lose control, we are losing control of the part of our brain that is responsible for logical reasoning and impulse control. Hence, it is no longer possible to logically reason our way out.
>
> An Autistic persons actions during a meltdown are not an indication of their usual character or personality; that part of their brain is not operating as usual.

> **If possible**, person who is losing control should be guided to a safe location, preferably with privacy, and / or bystanders should be redirected.
>
> Support the person to stay safe and minimise the risk of potential harm. **Stay calm.**

❹ Meltdown Stage

It's happening. The "emotional brain" is in control now. **This is fight or flight.** Signs may include:

- *becoming highly reactive*
- *struggling to communicate*
- *yelling, screaming or crying*
- *flopping to the floor*
- *an increase in stimming*
- *self-harming (e.g. scratching skin, hitting head)*
- *becoming physically aggressive*

⑤ De-escalating Stage

After the peak of the meltdown has passed, a person will start to de-escalate and the "emotional brain" will take a back-seat, and the "thinking brain" will start to operate as usual again.

During the de-escalation stage you may notice a person begin to:

- *breathe in their usual rhythm*

- *appear tired or worn out*

- *display signs of guilt and shame*

- *return to a more usual (for the individual) pattern of behaviour, body language and communication*

> Meltdowns can be mentally and physically exhausting, so although it may seem never ending, **it won't / can't last forever**; the nervous system will eventually calm down / wear out.

⑥ Recovery Stage

After the meltdown has finished, and the person may feel more like "themself" again or they might be completely drained. The following strategies can support recovery:

- *supporting opportunities for rest - encouraging a nap if needed*

- *reassuring them that you care for them and that your relationship is the same, reducing shame and guilt*

- *finding and offering comfort items, people and activities (e.g. favourite plushie, movies, parent / friends, art)*

> Be sure to wait for signs of recovery as re-escalation (another meltdown) is possible if demands, such as communication or activities, are imposed too early.

> Sunny Spectrum Supports Regulate, Connect and Support Guide.

Shutdowns

Shutdowns are similar to meltdowns in that they are involuntary, can have similar triggers, and have the same nervous system response. However, the outward presentation is different.

Shutdowns are more of a "retreat" from surroundings. They are often described as an "internalised meltdown" or being a "muted meltdown", as it is still an intense reaction to overload, overwhelm, or stress. In fact, shutdowns can indicate higher/more prolonged levels of stress to the nervous system. Likewise, they can take longer to recover from.

Signs of a shutdown may include:

WITHDRAWAL

Reduced enthusiasm for enjoyable activities or social engagements

UNRESPONSIVE

Reduced communication or changes to usual communication, dissociation, passive demeanour (often misinterpreted as apathy)

PHYSICAL SYMPTOMS

Fatigue, tension headache, reduced coordination, slowing of body movements

Reframing Autism: Emotional Regulation, Part Two: Using Co-regulation to Teach Emotional Regulation:
https://reframingautism.org.au/emotional-regulation-part-two-using-co-regulation-to-teach-emotional-regulation/

Reframing Autism: All about Autistic shutdown: Guide for allies.
https://reframingautism.org.au/all-about-Autistic-shutdown-guide-for-allies/

"When I have a shut-down meltdown, I do not have a choice about whether I speak or not, my body simply won't allow it."
- Autistic Adult

Shutdowns can be equally as distressing as meltdowns. While internalised, shutdowns don't mean that someone needs any less support than someone having externalised meltdowns. An individual may experience both shutdowns and meltdowns at different times and in different situations.

Now that you know why it happens...

Let's take a look at some practical strategies that you can try to support someone who is experiencing a meltdown or shutdown:

- **Reduce expectations/demands.**

- **Stay in close proximity** as this can bring comfort (co-regulation) - unless the individual has asked to be alone.

- **Use clear, calm and minimal communication** (don't forget that you can use AAC, sign, or even a simple "thumbs up" or "thumbs down") to reduce communication demands.

- **Be aware of sensory needs** and alter sensory scape as per the individuals needs (e.g. turn lights off, reduce noise).

- **Help meet sensory needs safely** (e.g. if head banging, offer a pillow as an alternative).

- **Showing care and understanding.** Validate and acknowledge current experience and feelings to avoid shame.

- **Offer comfort items where safe** (e.g. their special teddy or sensory item).

- **Tuning in to, and providing, the level of contact that is helpful for the individual** (it could be a hug, maybe texting instead of talking, doing an activity together that doesn't require talking, or perhaps even just knowing you are in a nearby room thinking about them).

Ultimately, the goal is to create an environment that communicates to the person's nervous system that they are safe. This can be achieved through non-speaking communication *(tone of voice, facial expression)* and attitude.

> **Some points to keep in mind:**
>
> - Never touch someone who is having a meltdown without permission -it can feel painful or threatening to a heightened nervous system
>
> - A meltdown is *not* a tantrum and people who experience meltdowns do *not* choose to behave this way
>
> - Every person has different techniques for getting through or preventing a meltdown – different coping mechanisms will work for different people
>
> **Shouting, judgmental stares, pointing, laughing, or negative comments are known to always be <u>unhelpful</u>.**

Empathy for others, and empathy for self, are associated with a calm nervous system.

SO, BY BEING CARING TOWARDS AN AUTISTIC PERSON YOU ARE MORE LIKELY TO BE ABLE TO CO-REGULATE THEIR NERVOUS SYSTEM.

Repeated exposure to distressing experiences can negatively impact mental health, as it builds on the narrative of distress cycles and adds to negative associations with those experiences.

One study found that Autistic individuals exhibit lower levels of self-compassion compared to non-Autistic people. The same study discovered that the degree of understanding and acceptance Autistic individuals receive from others influences their own self-compassion.

Self-compassion is a protective factor for wellbeing and depression prevention. So, as a supporter of an Autistic person experiencing distress, by simply showing compassion you can help to re-write the stories of "not being good enough" or "being too much".

AUTISTIC MASKING

The concept of masking has been briefly touched on, now lets take a closer look at what it is, and why it is important to understand.

Autistic masking, also known as camouflaging or adaptive morphing *(like a chameleon)*, describes behaving in a way to "act non-Autistic".

Even non-Autistic people "mask" to a degree. **For example**:

- Someone who has anxiety around public speaking may "mask" to give the impression that they are a confident speaker

- Someone may suppress their emotions *(such as sadness or frustration)* to maintain an upbeat demeanour

- Someone may mimic body language or expressions to fit in a social group

Now imagine having to hold up that mask all of the time.

Exhausting, right?

Masking can come in 3 variations:

COMPENSATION
Actions taken to compensate for differences

- *rehearsing*
- *studying*
- *planning*

CONCEALING
Actions taken to hide differences

- *supressing*
- *monitoring*
- *forcing*

ASSIMILATION
Actions aimed at blending in

- *mimicking*
- *performing*
- *following*

In one study, 70% of Autistic adults reported consistently engaging in masking.

Why do so many Autistic people mask?

For many people, masking is an experience of obligation, rather than a choice. Often, it is motivated by avoiding being isolated and ostracised, or even attacked. It can be both a survival mechanism and a trauma response.

Some people find masking advantageous, for example, someone may be able to achieve goals like receiving an education and maintaining a job, as well as establishing relationships with non-Autistic people.

THE PROBLEM IS... AUTISTIC MASKING IS DIRECTLY LINKED TO HIGHER LEVELS OF BURNOUT, DEPRESSION, ANXIETY, AND <u>SUICIDALITY</u>.

Then why not unmask?

Often, it is not as simple as "taking the mask on and off", remembering that this is a **survival mechanism**. It's about safety! Autistic people need safe spaces free from discrimination and judgement, and go through this journey on their own terms.

Sometimes, a person has been masking for so long they don't even know who they are without it, and this can be a whole other process to safely rediscover their authentic selves.

> **To support an Autistic person to unmask:**
>
> - Accept them as they are
> - Address inclusion
> - Be a consistent "safe person"

BURNOUT

You might be familiar with the term "occupational burnout" which refers to exhaustion due to prolonged work stress. Autistic Burnout is also a result of prolonged stress, however it arises for different reasons including mental overload and demands exceeding capacity.

Reasons for burnout include:

MASKING

Sustained demands of hiding/camouflaging Autistic traits in order to present non-Autistically

INTERPERSONAL INTERACTIONS

Sustained demands of modifying communication styles, use of non preferred communication styles (e.g. phone calls over text)

UNACCOMMODATING ENVIRONMENTS

Sustained demands of operating in unaccommodating environments

Autistic burnout can be debilitating, resulting in mental and physical exhaustion, increased sensitivity, overload and difficulty with regulation *(including meltdowns)*. An episode of burnout may be "acute" *(lasting a matter of hours or a few days)* or a "chronic" phase *(lasting months, even years)*. It is often mistaken for depression, however there are differentiating factors.

Social interaction, planning and even basic tasks can become more overwhelming. It can also trigger other conditions such as depression, insomnia, chronic pain, gastrointestinal issues, or worse, mental health crisis *(suicidality)*.

Autistic burnout occurs when a person has hit **'empty'**, drawn on all their energy reserves and they feel as though they are completely "depleted". At this point, it is much harder to 'mask' Autistic traits.

> Understanding burnout is helpful, as it is frequently triggered by expectations and pressures from other people. **This includes pressures to plan, mask, contribute and adjust.**
>
> Individuals experiencing burnout should not be urged to exceed their current limits. Instead, rest, compassion, patience, and support are required during this time, until they have regained their capacity.

4

ACCESSIBILITY

External: On the outside

ENVIRONMENTS

Environmental factors play a large role in how an Autistic person may or may not, be able to participate. When an environment is not accommodating, a common coping strategy is avoidance.

This means that many Autistic individuals are not participating in their communities which can significantly impact wellbeing.

There are 6 principles on how disabling or enabling an environment is:

SENSORY SCAPE

Sensory burden, sustained and inescapable input, uncontrollable environment

SPACE

Busy, crowded and/or confined spaces

PREDICTABILITY

Lack of information, inconsistent or unfamiliar situations

UNDERSTANDING

Unsupportive people, misunderstanding, judgement

ADJUSTMENTS

Unsuitable adjustments, pace pressures, inflexible communication

RECOVERY

No space to escape, unable to recover and prepare

Controlling the sensory environment can enable meaningful participation.

Sunny Spectrum Supports Regulate, Connect and Support Guide.

Common examples of disabling environments:

SHOPPING CENTRES

Bright lights, crowded space, forced small talk / inflexible communication, inescapable sensory input, unpredictable / uncontrollable environment, no calm space to regulate

HEALTHCARE

Need to communicate when in distress / pain, sensitivity to touch, strong smells, medical trauma, inflexible communication, poor / outdated knowledge

CAFES & RESTAURANTS

Loud coffee machines, overlapping noises, dishes clanging, forced small talk, different smells, unfamiliar menu choices, dietary restrictions, bright lights

SUPERMARKETS

Bright lights, beeping registers, loud store announcements, lots of people, manoeuvring a trolley, forced small talk / inflexible communication

CLUBS, STADIUMS, CONCERTS

Disorienting darkness, bright / flashing lights, loud sounds, confined spaces, unpredictable environment, pressure to socialise, no calm space to regulate

PUBLIC TRANSPORT

Crowded space, confined smells, unexpected sounds and vibrations, unpredictable route, navigating unfamiliar places, transitioning between services

One study found that outdoor spaces, cinemas, clubs, and stadiums are less disabling than the other environments mentioned.

Activities at these venues often align with interests, and attendees likely know (and perhaps even love) what they are signing up to. They may even seek the particular sensory input ("**Sensory-Yum**" or sensory "**Glimmer**"). In contrast, other environments can be less predictable and less aligned with interests, both sensory-wise and socially.

Why is this important?

Autistic people may avoid participating in some environments, which can be detrimental to wellbeing.

For example:

- Avoiding shopping centres may result in reduced access to food
- Avoiding health care settings may result in poor health outcomes
- Avoiding recreation areas may result in someone being isolated

Reducing the burden of sensory input can be an enabling factor for participation.

A good example of this is "quiet hours" at supermarkets.

Quieter hours for shopping with reduced music in stores, reduced cash register sounds, lower lighting and less traffic of people may allow people with sensory sensitivity to participate in that environment, hence having better access to nutritious food.

What can you do?

We don't all have the opportunity to change "big environments" like shopping centres, but we can all be more mindful.

Everyone has the opportunity to support a sensory experience by:

Offering to help someone to navigate the environment, especially finding an exit or quiet space if overwhelmed

Removing pace pressures, such as being patient when someone is ordering, and flexibility with communication

Offering warning if you can predict a big sensory input ("this machine will make a loud beep when...")

If you're a manager or decision maker, you could also consider:

Sound
Exploring quiet hour options or lowering other sounds such as cash registers and music.

Lighting
Avoiding overly bright lights like fluorescent down-lights can be helpful for many Autistic individuals.

Space
Where possible, providing adequate room to move around.

Predictability
Providing sensory maps and visual directions in accessibility information.

Clarity
Displaying clear signage and easy to read directions to reduce potential for confusion or panic.

Understanding
Having staff trained in Autism access and support.

Breaks
Where possible offering calm spaces that people can use to regulate so they don't have to leave if overwhelmed.

Tools
If practical, offering tools like fidgets or ear plugs that visitors can borrow.

> **Sometimes environments can't be changed, but they can be made predictable. Often, small things go a long way, such as when entering a room asking *"How is the lighting for you? Shall we turn the lights off or keep them on?"*.**
>
> It's a good idea to ask everyone these questions, not just people who you know are Autistic.

Social Stories™

Social stories are a tool that an establishment can use to provide beneficial information for people to successfully navigate an environment they might not have been before. They are a narrative with descriptive and directive sentences alongside images. These images can be actual images of the establishment or a generic image to match the text. Social stories can reduce the unpredictability aspect of going to a new place.

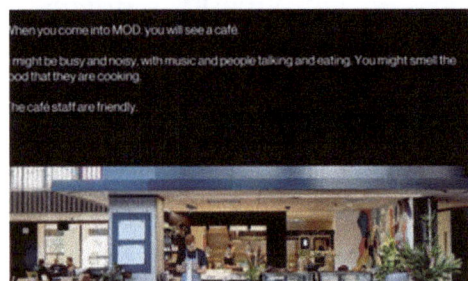

Sensory Maps

Sensory maps are visuals that help people understand and navigate sensory environments. They typically depict different sensory stimuli in a particular space, such as lights, sounds, textures, and smells, to help people anticipate and manage sensory experiences on where to expect different sensory elements.

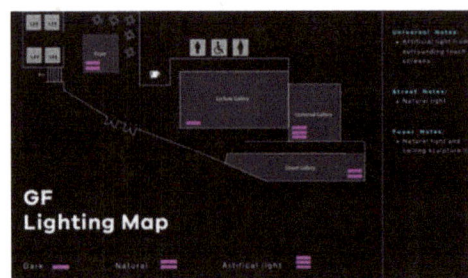

"Social Stories" by Carol Gray.
https://carolgraysocialstories.com/

COMMUNICATION

Communication is one of the most fundamental aspects of human interaction. While the first thing you think of might be talking with "mouth words", in reality, communication encompasses a wide range of processes that contribute to understanding, connection, and effective exchange of information between people.

There are many cues that help us understand what another person is communicating. It is not just what someone says that helps us understand, but it is how they say it, their expression, body language, gestures and the context in which they're saying it.

Some Autistic people may not hold eye contact or use body language in expected ways. They may misunderstand or misuse gestures or have different facial expressions.

Some Autistic people may also have an unexpected tone, repeat certain phrases, mainly talk about their interests, use other means of communication (e.g. AAC) or have other differences in how they verbally communicate.

These differences can make social interactions challenging between Autistic and non-Autistic people, and sometimes confusing when trying to meet in the middle!

EVERYONE HAS THE RIGHT TO COMMUNICATE IN A WAY THAT WORKS FOR THEM.

THE COMMUNICATION BILL OF RIGHTS APPLIES TO ALL PEOPLE WITH AND WITHOUT DISABILITIES.

https://www.communicationhub.com.au/CommunicationHub/Communication_Hub/Communication_is_a_human_right/Communication_is_essential.aspx

COMMUNICATION:
Expressive

Expressive communication is the way someone uses languages to express themselves. Common methods include:

SPEECH / MOUTH WORDS

AUGMENTATIVE AND ALTERNATIVE COMMUNICATION (AAC) DEVICE

WRITING

DRAWING

GESTURES

BODY LANGUAGE

AAC is a common way for Autistic people to communicate. It encompasses all non-speaking ways of communication, including those above. Someone who uses AAC may have a specific device, which could be electronic or print based.

REMEMBER, JUST BECAUSE SOMEONE MAY NOT BE USING MOUTH WORDS, DOESN'T MEAN THEY DON'T HAVE ANYTHING TO SAY.

https://www.speechpathologyaustralia.org.au/Public/Public/Comm-swallow/Aug-alt-strategies/Augmentative-Alternative-Communication.aspx

https://thespectrum.org.au/autism-strategy/autism-strategy-communication/

Here are some tips for respectful communication with an AAC user:

- **Give the person time and don't interrupt unnecessarily.** Constructing messages with AAC may take longer.

- **Be patient and allow the person to complete their thoughts.** Interrupting can disempower the AAC user.

- **Some AAC users may have a communication partner to support them.** If this occurs, still direct your communication with the user rather than communication partner. That person is an aid, not a replacement.

- **Respect their personal space and equipment.**

- If you feel inclined to assist such as holding the device at a better angle or navigating to a different screen – **you must explicitly ask first.**

- **Treat adults as adults.** Always presume competence.

- **Speak in your natural/usual tone.** Adjusting your speaking style unnecessarily, like talking louder or slower, can come across as patronising.

Basically, treat the individual how you would treat any other person.

AAC is for anyone; adults, children, and even individuals that use spoken language but occasionally may become non-speaking in an overwhelming situation.

https://spokenaac.com/blog/proper-aac-etiquette/

Some common, but non-standard, verbal expressions you might encounter...

ECHOLALIA

The repetition of words or sounds. It can be used as a way to communicate as well as a way to self-soothe, or even to talk oneself through completing a difficult task.

VOCAL STIMS

Could include humming, singing, whistling, counting out loud, or tongue clicking, among others.

TICS

Sudden and repetitive sounds or movements someone makes involuntarily.

> *"Vocal stimming is one of my favourite ways to regulate. Sometimes it happens subconsciously, other times I will turn the music up in my headphones and "let it all out". The energy release feels cathartic."*
> **- Autistic Adult**

When someone engages in vocal stimming, it serves a purpose for them. Please avoid interrupting or telling them to be quiet.

https://www.neurodiverging.com/introduction-to-echolalia-and-Autistic-scripting/

https://psychcentral.com/autism/autism-tics#next-steps

COMMUNICATION:
Receptive

Receptive communication refers to how someone understands language.

It involves the ability to comprehend spoken words, written text, and non-verbal cues such as gestures and facial expressions. Receptive communication is essential for effective interactions, as it allows us to process information, follow instructions, and engage meaningfully in conversations.

Ways that people receive messages can include:

HEARING

VISUAL CUES

READING

BODY LANGUAGE

SIGN LANGUAGE / AUSLAN

DIGITAL MEDIA

Autistic people may receive and process this information differently than the neurotypical. This might include:

- *literal interpretation of language*

- *preference or need for direct communication*

- *needing additional processing time (time needed can vary greatly)*

- *differences in use and understanding of non-verbal cues*

- *different use of pragmatics (i.e. starting and stopping conversation, knowing when it's your turn etc.)*

- *differences in using and recognising facial expressions*

- *differences in the filtering of important vs. unimportant information*

Various Autistic experiences can interfere with communication. For example, sensory overload, meltdown or shutdown can affect the ability to process information and access communication.

SENSORY OVERLOAD   **SHUTDOWN**   **MELTDOWN**

In these situations the brain prioritises the fight or flight response, which can lead to a decrease in both receptive and expressive language capabilities. This is because the area of the brain that is responsible for processing communication can't be accessed at the time.

Communication tips...

Every Autistic person is different. However, what is usually favoured:

SAY WHAT YOU MEAN, AND MEAN WHAT YOU SAY

This will reduce the likelihood of communication breakdowns. Direct and sincere exchanges pave the way for more meaningful connections and successful outcomes.

- **Discuss with the person directly about how they prefer to be communicated with** (or ask their support person).

- **Be aware of your own communication style and how you use spoken words.** Be mindful of different processing styles/abilities. You may need to slow down and allow more processing time.

- If you suspect an individual has not understood or processed what you have said, **modify your language.**(e.g. clearer and simplified instructions).

- **Be specific and intentional with questions** and support understanding of what is not explicitly stated.

- **Provide specific descriptions and steps. Autistic** people benefit from context and knowing "why".

- When asking someone to do something, break it down into **"first this, then that"**. (e.g., first put your shoes on, then tie the laces).

- **Use pictures and written information** to compliment instructions/ directions/ conversation.

https://www.amaze.org.au/wp-content/uploads/2019/06/Amaze-Information-Sheet-How-to-communicate-your-message-to-people-on-the-autism-spectrum.pdf

Autistic people can often take things on "face value" and can't always read between the lines.

Avoid things like...

AMBIGUITY
IDIOMS
METAPHORS
SARCASM
NON-LITERAL LANGUAGE

- *Asking questions that can have multiple meanings or multiple responses, that are dependent on context.*

- *Using vague or conceptual descriptions – e.g. "he was salty" rather than "he was angry".*

- *Multi-step verbal instructions or directions; particularly if the person appears distracted by the environment.*

- *Surprises or changes to routine without forewarning or appropriate supports to cope with change.*

- **Metaphors:** *e.g. "time is money", "double edged sword"*
  Comparing two dissimilar things might be confusing

- **Idioms:** *"bite the bullet", "the ball is in your court"*
  Abstract use of language might be hard to relate to

- **Sarcasm:** *"ask me if I care", "good luck with that"*
  This may be interpreted as a genuine, missing the point

https://thespectrum.org.au/autism-strategy/autism-strategy-communication/

https://drroseann.com/neurotypical-vs-neurodivergent-communication-embracing-diversity-in-dialogue/

COMMUNICATION BARRIERS

Communication difficulties often arise between Autistic and non-Autistic individuals due to differences in communication styles and information processing styles.

When both parties communicate in their natural manner, it can become challenging for them to understand each other, leading to communication breakdowns. According to Milton's **Double Empathy Problem**, these difficulties and breakdowns stem not from deficits in Autistic individuals, but from a *mutual* mismatch in communication styles. However, the blame often tends to fall on the Autistic person. This can be attributed to societal expectations and the stigma attached to the Autistic experience, as seen in the deficit-focused diagnostic criteria (i.e., the DSM).

Non-Autistic communication and ways of expressing empathy are generally considered the expected "social norm," and most people view the neurotypical way as "correct." This means that when Autistic people communicate in unexpected ways, it is viewed as "abnormal" or "wrong."

Milton suggests that:

NEITHER THE AUTISTIC OR THE NEUROTYPICAL PERSON ARE AT FAULT; RATHER, THEY ARE SIMPLY MISINTERPRETING EACH OTHER.

This type of communication breakdown can be described as similar to speaking "two different languages".

No one is right or wrong, neither language is "better", it is just different.

It is crucial to understand that neither communication style is inherently "right" or "wrong," contrary to common misconceptions.

The assumption that the non-Autistic way is inherently "*correct*" has a profound impact, often resulting in natural disadvantages for Autistic people.

When non-Autistic individuals view neurotypical social ideals as the only way to demonstrate empathy, it creates an expectation for Autistic people to adapt to non-Autistic culture and communication norms *(leading to masking)*.

Consider "social skills training" that is typically designed to help Autistic children socialise with neurotypical children. It's notable that this same effort isn't commonly applied to non-Autistic children's' understanding of Autistic social skills. Consequently, it could be argued that non-Autistic individuals may lack empathy in understanding Autistic individuals.

One study showed that Autistic people communicate effectively with one another, and that difficulties only arise with non-Autistic people, and vice versa. This challenges the deficit focussed autism diagnostic criteria that suggests Autistic people lack the skills to successfully interact!

This concept is important because it challenges the idea that Autistic people lack theory of mind, and it reframes the disconnect between Autistic and non-Autistic communities.

Non-Autistic people can experience different ranges of empathy (empathetic to unempathetic) - so can Autistic people! "Autistic empathy" is no less compassionate, it might just look different.

There is no need to think of superior and inferior ways of connecting, we can just accept our co-existence has natural differences.

Reframing Autism. (n.d.). Milton's double empathy problem: A summary for non-academics.
https://reframingautism.org.au/miltons-double-empathy-problem-a-summary-for-non-academics/

5

CONNECTION

Bringing it together

INTERNAL AND EXTERNAL COMING TOGETHER

This handbook has discussed how Autistic people navigate the world through a unique interplay of internal and external factors.

For example:

INTERNAL

*Processing information differently
(sensory and cognitive)
Passionate interests
Different thinking styles*

EXTERNAL

*Unsuitable environments
Communication breakdowns
Societal expectations
Perpetuated myths*

The dynamic interaction between internal sensory-cognitive experiences and external environmental and social factors creates a complex landscape through which Autistic individuals navigate.

Autistic people don't experience their internal self and their external environments in isolation; it is a combination of these coming together.

It is now clear why the main drivers of poor outcomes, relate to _external_ factors, including:

- *poor understanding within the community and among service providers*

- *unaccommodating environments; and*

- *a complex and poorly integrated service system*

ACCESSIBILITY PROMOTES INCLUSION, AND INCLUSION PROMOTES BETTER OUTCOMES

What inaccessibility can lead to:

An exclusion cycle begins to progress when an Autistic person is using their energy to participate, and then:

They may start to feel overwhelmed, especially when they don't have access to accommodations.

From there, they may move to a state of hypersensitivity and a state of survival where the nervous system is dysregulated.

As a result, they might need more support to maintain their health and wellbeing, as well as to care for themselves and their families.

If these additional needs are not met, they may experience more vulnerability as a result of hypersensitivity, meltdowns, shutdowns and burnout. For some, this may feel like exposure as they have been "unmasked" without choice or safety. This can be isolating and lead that person to feel vulnerable and exposed.

Whilst dysregulated, unaccommodated with increasing need for support, being exposed may invoke a sense of shame or helplessness if the cycle continues. They may question if they truly belong.

Without change, the cycle begins again, with even more energy being used to try to fit into a world that isn't accommodating, and further experiences of stigma and isolation contribute to exclusion.

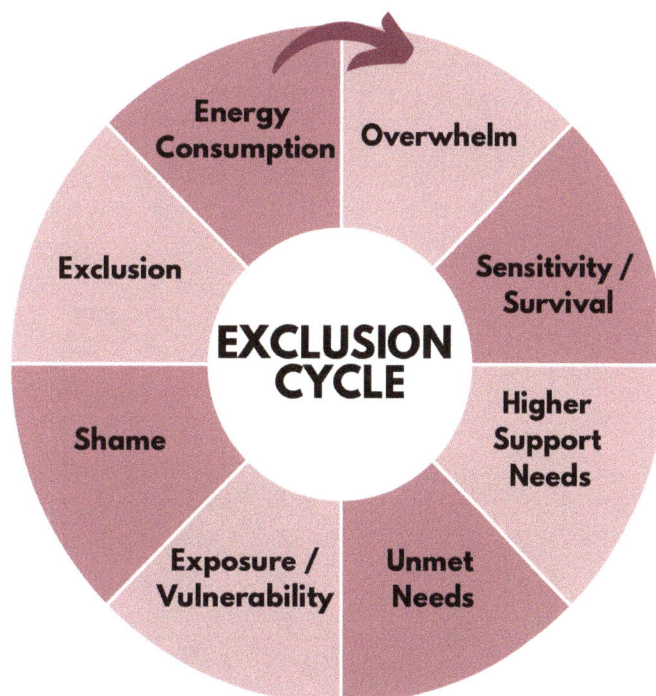

Energy Consumption · **Overwhelm** · **Sensitivity / Survival** · **Higher Support Needs** · **Unmet Needs** · **Exposure / Vulnerability** · **Shame** · **Exclusion**

EXCLUSION CYCLE

On the other hand...

When Autistic people experience supportive and accommodating environments, **the cycle is now one of inclusion**. In this model, energy consumption is the same as the exclusion model due to existing in a wider world that isn't designed for Autistic people.

Only now...

⬆ The environment is accommodating in a way that is flexible and suited to different sensory and communication needs.

⬆ Accommodations mean the individual may feel more regulated and have more *stable* support needs.

⬆ Therefore, they can access to the usual level of support they require to be experience meaningful inclusion and participation.

⬆ Individuals have a safe environment with the opportunity "unmask" and be their authentic selves and are met with acceptance for who they are.

⬆ This has the likelihood of resulting in less shame and sense of belonging in their community.

🔄 This alternative cycle fosters an environment of inclusion, and Autistic individuals do not have to dedicate as much energy into navigating an inaccessible and exclusive world.

INCLUSION CYCLE: Energy Consumption, Accommodation, Regulation, Stablised Support Needs, Needs Met, Authenticity, Acceptance, Inclusion

When someone is met "where they're at", and community members align to neuro-affirming ways of connection, inclusion is promoted over exclusion.

Remember, the person is not the problem. If you accept an Autistic person and their uniqueness, it will support them to feel a sense of safety and they will be more likely to share their authentic self with you, be appreciated for who they are, and live a better life!

You won't always *(and don't always)* need to know a persons support or access needs, but you will *always* have the opportunity to be an accessible person.

The information provided in this handbook aims to empower you to offer support and accommodations that can significantly benefit the Autistic community.

By simply offering someone options *(such as alternate seating or lighting)*, demonstrating awareness and readiness to be a safe person, you are more likely to become a safe person to discuss their access needs with. Even if someone doesn't want or need what you offer, it sets the scene for them to share their preferences because you are an approachable and safe person.

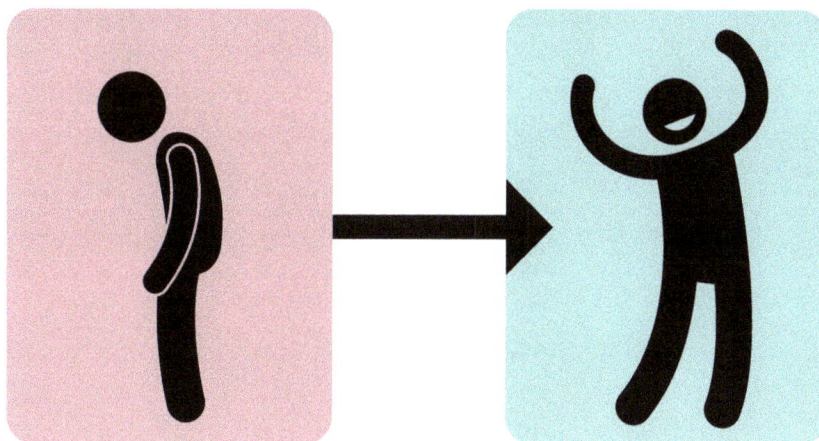

An expanded summary of tips and strategies is included in the Regulate, Connect and Support Guide provided on page 45.

Autistic individuals can also use these tips to advocate for their needs or to support themselves independently!

MYTH BUSTING

Now that you're equipped with more knowledge about autism, you should see why the following myths are untrue:

1. "Autism wasn't a thing in my day"

Just because someone didn't have the label, doesn't mean that they weren't Autistic. For example, someone may be labelled as "weird", "naughty" or "quirky", and may have been bullied as a child or had difficulty in school but the language around autism was not yet there.

Many misconceptions about Autistic behaviours still exist, and barriers to diagnosis and support persist. However, our understanding of autism has expanded significantly, supported by a wealth of research and a growing number of voices from those with lived experience, particularly adults who can reflect over generations.

> Did you know that Autism was not included in the Diagnostic and Statistical Manual (DSM) until 1980. Likewise, until 2013 there was no possibility of a dual diagnosis of Autism and ADHD. Diagnosticians were only able to diagnose one or the other; whereas now we know that more often than not, they co-occur

2. "It's attention seeking" or "bad parenting"

External behaviour is often a form of communication with an underlying cause/need. Children aren't immune from overwhelm and adults are not childish if they communicate unmet needs with behaviours.

Parenting is not the cause or a 'cure' for autism.

> Reframe your thinking from "Autistic people are attention seeking", to "Autistic people are support seeking".

3. "Vaccines cause Autism"

Based upon fabricated research, this has long since been disproven and retracted in 2010. The fraudulent researcher's name was Andrew Wakefield.

> https://www.unicef.org/montenegro/en/stories/mmr-vaccine-does-not-cause-autism

> There is a substantial body of research showing that autism is largely genetic.
>
> **Looking at family history, Autistic traits can often be seen in relatives, perhaps without the attached stigma.**
>
> Understanding autism in this way can help us foster greater acceptance within our communities.

4. "They'd make great friends, they're both Autistic"

Yes, many Autistic people have shared experiences, but like neurotypical individuals, they are all diverse and have their own strengths, interests, challenges, circumstances, privileges, values, goals, and dreams.

Though there may be similarities in communication styles in some cases, each Autistic person is unique and a shared neurotype doesn't automatically mean that they will be best friends or "get along" in a social group.

5. "They're good with computers, math, and science"

Some people are. But like everyone, Autistic people have a wide variety of talents, interests, and strengths. The diversity in abilities reflects how unique each Autistic person is, and that they should not be confined to narrow expectations and stereotypes associated with their neurotype.

6. "It's a childhood thing"

Autistic children grow into Autistic adults, and they always have!

However, now we have more awareness/knowledge about autism, better understanding about misdiagnoses, and diverse community representation and visibility.

Autism is a lifelong natural variation. Just as neurotypical individuals develop and change over time, so do Autistic individuals, with their **Autistic neurotype** remaining an integral part of how they process and experience the world around them.

> Diagnosis as a child is more accessible than diagnosis as an adult.
>
> Greater awareness means that traits in children are often detected at childcare or school. Whereas, adults who don't fit the "stereotype" have often faced lifelong barriers resulting in exclusion and often subsequent mental health conditions.
>
> There are no public/free diagnostic pathways as an adult, and private assessments are costly with long waiting lists in Australia.

7. "They don't have empathy"

Just like neurotypical people, Autistic people exhibit a wide range of empathy levels and unique ways of expressing it. Empathy might be demonstrated through actions rather than words, or through intense emotional sensitivity that can sometimes lead to withdrawal as a coping mechanism.

Misunderstandings often arise from differences in communication styles, rather than from a lack of empathy. Reflect on the "Double Empathy Problem".

> How many unempathetic neurotypical people have you met?

8. "Only little boys are Autistic"

In the past, Autistic individuals were typically perceived as Anglo-Saxon, white, male children, especially those with speech and/or intellectual disabilities. This was due to the narrow framing of diagnostic criteria and a limited understanding of diverse presentations.

Today, our understanding of autism has significantly broadened, leading to better access to diagnosis and a deeper recognition of various aspects of the autistic experience, such as masking, internalised presentations, and sensory sensitivities.

However, there is still work to be done in ensuring that those with intersectional identities and co-occurring conditions receive the acknowledgement and support they need.

9. "Autistic people don't talk or live everyday lives; if they do they're just mildly Autistic or have Asperger's"

This is an oversimplification of the Autistic experience.

Autism is a "spectrum" meaning that there are many ways that a person might present. Reflect on the history of functioning labels and why this language is used.

> **Asperger's and autism are the same thing.**
>
> Asperger's was removed from the Diagnostic and Statistical Manual (DSM) in 2013 and was merged with "Autism Spectrum" due to the overlap in "symptoms". This improved diagnostic accuracy, consistency, and access to necessary resources and support for more Autistic people.
>
> **It is also important to note that speech and/or intellectual disabilities are separate to autism. They can often co-occur, but not every Autistic person has these additional disabilities.**

6

RESOURCES

GLOSSARY

Ableism: the discrimination of and social prejudice against people with disabilities based on the belief that non-disabled people are superior.

Attention Deficit Hyperactivity Disorder (ADHD): the diagnostic term for people with significant differences in executive functioning (see 'executive functioning').

Attitudinal environment: the collective attitudes, beliefs, perceptions, and biases held by people and society that influence how people think, feel, and behave toward others.

Augmentative and Alternative Communication (AAC): describes various means of communication that augments (adds to or enhances) or provides an alternative to speech or mouth words.

Adjustments / accommodations: changes to the environment and/or expectations to improve inclusion.

AuDHD: a term coined by the community of Autistic people with co-existing ADHD to describe, and embrace, their identity. Some people describe themselves as "AuDHDers".

Autistic Burnout: a state of chronic exhaustion, loss of functioning, sensory sensitivity and an inability to mask. It is experienced by Autistic people after prolonged periods with insufficient accommodations.

Communication: the exchange of information through speaking, writing or AAC.

GLOSSARY

Cognitive / Cognition: conscious mental processes such as thinking reasoning and remembering.

Co-regulation: deliberate strategies used by a person to help another person achieve a sense of calm and safety, to support the regulation of their nervous systems.

Double empathy problem: a theory first explored by Dr Damien Milton in 2012 which explains that communication breakdowns are the result of a lack of empathy and understanding by both Autistic and non-Autistic people. The theory emphasises that communication is a 'two way street' and is the responsibility of both communication partners.

DSM-5-TR (DSM): the Diagnostic and Statistical Manual of Mental Disorders, 5th Edition. Used by mental health practitioners in the diagnosis of mental health conditions and autism.

Echolalia: repetition of words or phrases, can be used for learning language or stimming.

Emotional contagion: an experience where a person's emotions and related behaviours trigger similar emotions and behaviours in others around them.

Glimmer: the opposite of a "trigger" for our nervous system. They are small moments of joy, safety, and connection that can make you feel safe and calm. They are often sensory based and may be called a "sensory yum".

sunny
spectrum supports

GLOSSARY

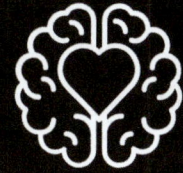

Hidden disability: a disability that is not visible or immediately apparent.

Hypersensitivity: <u>more</u> sensitive than typical to sensory stimuli.

Hyposensitivity: <u>less</u> sensitive than typical to sensory stimuli.

Infantilise: to treat someone as a child or in a way that denies their maturity in age or experience.

Institutional environment: the frameworks, policies, procedures, and cultural attitudes within an organisation that influences how it operates.

Internalised ableism: see "ableism". Experienced by individuals with disabilities who internalise negative stereotypes, beliefs, and attitudes about disability that are prevalent in society.

Intersectional Identity: refers to a person or group who identify with more than one community affected by marginalisation/oppression. E.g. Black and Autistic.

Interoception: the awareness of body sensations and cues that provide information about bodily needs and functions including thirst, hunger and pain.

LGBTQIA+: acronym for Lesbian, Gay, Bisexual, Transgender, Queer, Intersex, Asexual (or Agender or Aromantic). The '+' includes anyone who doesn't identify with the specific terms.

sunny
spectrum supports

GLOSSARY

Masking/Camouflaging: the act of concealing or compensating for Autistic traits by internalising natural experiences.

Meltdowns: a external presentation of distress, overload and overwhelm which an individual experiences involuntarily.

Monotropic Focus: the tendency to deeply focus on a single interest or activity to the exclusion of other stimuli, like "tunnel vision".

Nervous system: the brain, spinal cord and the bodies system of nerves that provide information about the state of our bodies and controls how the body reacts to perceived threats.

Neuro-affirming: practices aligned with the neurodiversity movement. Practices that accept and embrace differences, whilst never attempting to discourage or 'fix' neurodivergent behaviour.

Neurodivergence: divergence from the most common/typical neurology and functioning.

Neurodivergent: a person or group whose mind and functioning differ from the most common/typical.

Neurodiversity (paradigm): an ideology which argues that neurodivergent brains are of equal value and worth as neurotypical brains.

Neurodiversity (movement): a social movement which actively works to create change in attitudes, systems and policy.

sunny
spectrum supports

GLOSSARY

Neurotypical: a person who whose ways of being align with typical expectations and who doesn't identify as neurodivergent.

Non-speaking: people who don't use mouth words to communicate.

Prefrontal cortex: part of the cerebral cortex, in the brain, responsible for higher order thinking. Helps plan complex cognition and behaviours, personality expression, decision making and is involved in executive functioning and regulation.

Proprioception: a sense responsible for our awareness of our bodies, their position in space and movement.

Same Foods / Safe Foods: a specific type or brand of food that is consistently eaten to provide a sense of comfort and predictability, reducing anxiety associated with mealtimes.

Sensory processing: refers to the way individuals perceive, organise and interpret sensory information.

Sensory Profile: an individual's sensory processing patterns and how these patterns affect their daily life. It helps identify how a person responds to sensory stimuli in their environment.

Shutdown: an internal presentation of distress, overload and overwhelm which an individual experiences involuntarily.

sunny
spectrum supports

Special Interests: interests or activities that bring Autistic people meaning, comfort, regulation, joy, knowledge, skills and community. Sometimes also referred to as "SpIn's" for short.

Stimming: functional repetitive behaviours that are used to self-soothe, regulate, express, communicate and more. Often Autistic and other neurodivergent people need to stim more than others.

Stigma: to negative attitudes and beliefs that society and individuals hold towards people due to their circumstances, characteristics or identities.

Tics: repetitive involuntary sudden movement or vocalisations, often related to tic disorder and Tourette syndrome.

Unmasking: the process of embracing ones' authentic self, freely exposing neurodivergent traits.

Vestibular system: the sensory system responsible for our awareness of balance and spatial orientation.

REGULATE

CONNECT & SUPPORT GUIDE

PRACTICAL STRATEGIES FOR ALLIES:
FOSTERING INCLUSION IN THE COMMUNITY

Regulate, Connect and Support Guide

This resource offers guiding principles and practical strategies for regulation. It is designed to enable effective communication and genuine connections, as well as to support Autistic individuals in managing their sensory experiences, regulating their nervous system, and enhancing their overall wellbeing.

This guide also includes tips for effectively supporting a person who may be dysregulated and experiencing a meltdown, or, nervous system response.

R espect communication styles

E ngage interests

G ive time to process and prepare

U nderstand sensory differences

L isten curiously

A sk about support needs

T ailor environments flexibly

E mbrace neurodiversity

Regulate, Connect and Support Guide

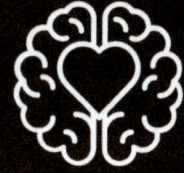

Respect communication styles

Clear & Direct Say what you mean and mean what you say.	**Avoid Ambiguity** E.g. "I'll meet you at lunch"... what time is your lunch and is it the same time?
Modify Language If you notice you have been misunderstood; clarify what you mean without judgement.	**Small Talk** Do not pressure someone to talk about their weekend or the weather if they seem disinterested in doing so.
AAC Users Constructing messages with AAC may take longer; don't interrupt. Respect personal space and equipment, treat adults as adults.	**Boundaries** Be mindful of comfort levels. If someone seems uncomfortable in continuing a conversation, respect boundaries and try again another time.
Understand People process and use non-verbal cues, pragmatics *(including interruptions)*, and facial expressions differently.	**Behaviour is Communication** Dysregulation could be an indication of an unmet a support need. When someone is dysregulated they may communicate differently.

Engage interests

Engage When relevant, engaging with an interest related activity can be a source of connection, even learning.	**Common Ground** Look for overlaps between a persons interests and yours. Some people may appreciate hearing about your interests to find a point of connection.
Show Genuine Interest Take the time to learn about people's interests. Ask questions and engage in conversations about their favourite topics. This can help build connection.	**Respect Expertise** Many Autistic people have deep knowledge about their interests. Acknowledge and appreciate this; you might learn something new!
Tools for Connection Interests can be a way to connect. Don't discourage them if you don't find them interesting, use them as a tool to connect.	**Don't Patronise** Treat adults as adults despite possibly having an interest you may view as "childish".

Regulate, Connect and Support Guide

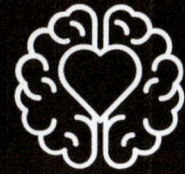

Give time to process and prepare

Allow Extra Time Be patient and give people plenty of time to process what has been said. Avoid rushing them to respond or complete tasks.	**Break Down Information** Present information in small, manageable chunks. This makes it easier to process and reduces the risk of feeling overwhelmed.
Use Visuals Create visuals such as "social stories and "sensory maps". Visual aids can help in predicting what will happen and reduce anxiety.	**Give Advance Notice** Whenever possible, provide information about upcoming changes in advance.
Explain things differently Be prepared to explain something in multiple ways to help someone understand what you're communicating.	**Encourage Questions** Let people know that it's ok to ask questions if they need clarification or more time to understand something.

Don't Patronise
Do not assume that someone is less intelligent if they process differently.

Regulate, Connect and Support Guide

Understand sensory differences

Everyone has a unique "sensory profile" and people may seek or avoid different types of sensory input.

Autistic people may use "stimming" to regulate their sensory system. Consider providing access to sensory items in relevant spaces.

Sensory Item Examples

Headphones/ear plugs, instruments, sound machines.	Projector lights, bubble tubes tinted glasses/sunglasses, liquid/glitter/sand motion items *(e.g. timer, lava lamp).*
Fidget toys, *(consider items that spin, stretch, squish and roll),* weighted items, blankets, cushions, soft toys, heated blanket.	Aroma therapy necklaces, scented items, nose plugs, diffusers, air purifiers.
Chewelry, crushed ice, silicone straws, flavoured candies, chewing gum.	Swings, wobble cushions, exercise balls, balance boards, rocking chairs, "crashmats".

Regulate, Connect and Support Guide

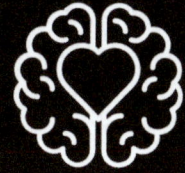

Listen curiously

Lived-Experience Listen to the lived-experiences of neurodivergent people to understand different perspectives.	**Disability** View from the social and human rights model *(what does this person need)* rather than the medical model *(what is wrong)*.
Assume Capability Always presume competence, listen to what people say and don't "infantilise".	**Acknowledge Feelings** E.g. "I can see that you're feeling overwhelmed right now. Would you like to take a break or find a quiet space?"
Respect Boundaries E.g. "If you need some time alone, just let me know. I'll be here when you're ready to talk."	**Check In** E.g. "How are you feeling about everything right now? Is there anything I can do to help?"
Recognise the complex interplay between a person's internal experience and external factors.	

Regulate, Connect and Support Guide

Ask about support needs

Time and Place
Respect confidentiality. It can be difficult to disclose needs. Consider a private setting where the person can feel safe and relaxed.

Be Specific
Ask about specific situations or triggers to better understand a person's needs. E.g. "When we're in crowded places, what can I do to help you feel more comfortable?"

Provide Options
E.g. Offer different ways to communicate needs, such as writing, drawing, or using assistive technology.

Sunflower
Recognise the use of the sunflower symbol (usually a lanyard) as a person disclosing their potential need for support.

Follow Up
Check in periodically to see if the someone's needs have changed or if there's anything new you can do to help.

Appreciate
It can be difficult to ask for support! Thank the person for sharing their needs and express your commitment to supporting them.

Recognise that many Autistic people mask their Autistic traits or support needs (often for your comfort, at a cost to them later).

Tailor environments flexibly

The ability to control aspects of the environment can enable meaningful participation. If environments can't be changed, they can be made predictable.

Consider universal design. Support strategies for Autistic people can benefit many other people too.

Sensory Scape Consider:	
Lighting Use natural light where possible, avoid harsh fluorescent lights, provide dimmer switches and low lighting zones. Consider normalising questions such as "How is the lighting for you? Shall we turn the lights off or keep them on?".	**Sound** Reduce sudden loud noises or provide warnings for sudden sounds, use soft music, use sound absorbing materials indoors, explore quiet hour options or lowering other sounds such as cash registers and music, provide noise cancelling headphones or earplugs.
Smell Avoid strong perfumes and air fresheners, ensure good ventilation (consider an air-purifier).	**Temperature** Provide options for temperature control. E.g. consider fans, blankets etc.

Regulate, Connect and Support Guide

Tailor environments flexibly

Space Ensure spaces are clear of clutter (physical or visual) so that people can easily move around.	**Predictability/Clarity** Provide "sensory maps" and "social stories" with visual directions and accessibility information, displaying clear signage and easy to read directions for easy navigation.
Understanding Having staff trained in autism access, inclusion and support.	**Accommodations** If practical, offering tools like fidgets or ear plugs that visitors can borrow.

Recovery
Where possible offer calm spaces that people can use to regulate so they don't have to leave if they are overwhelmed. If a specific sensory room is not possible, consider any quiet area away from the "hustle and bustle".

Embrace Neurodiversity

Labels Avoid referring to "functioning labels" *(e.g. high functioning / low functioning)*.	**Celebrate Strengths** Neurodivergent people bring unique skills and strengths.
Avoid Stereotyping Avoid making generalised assumptions. Always assume capability first.	**Encourage Self-Advocacy** Support individuals in advocating for their support needs.
Respect Identity Culture Model community preferences; "Autistic" person, not person "with autism".	**Neurodivergent Creators** Follow on social media, support businesses and artists.
Consider Intersectionality Intersectional identities, such as race, gender, disability, and socioecenomic status, interact and create unique experiences and challenges.	**Celebrate Neurodiversity** E.g. Through events, campaigns, awareness days and everyday acceptance to demonstrate that you are a safe-person.

Regulate, Connect and Support Guide

Supporting Dysregulation

Nervous system dysregulation can lead to meltdowns, shutdowns, avoidance and burnout.

When someone is overwhelmed or dysregulated the goal is to create an environment that communicates to the person's nervous system that they are safe.

Don't Touch Someone in meltdown or shutdown (unless they ask for this). Senses can be heightened and the person may be easily startled.	**Show Compassion** Assure the person that they are safe, that their response made sense and let them know that they are cared for.
Encourage Self-Compassion This helps nervous system regulation.	**Encourage Self-Advocacy** Support people to advocate for their support needs.
Environment Adapt the space to suit the person's sensory needs or support the person to move to an alternate place.	**Refer to Interests** Passions and interests are a great source of comfort and can support nervous system regulation (after the peak of a meltdown).

Regulate, Connect and Support Guide

Supporting Dysregulation

Demands Reduce demands, pressures and expectations until the person has regulated again.	**Reduce Communication** Use minimal communication as the person may struggle to process language at this time.
Comfort Items If you are aware of specific comfort items, provide these if it is safe to do so.	**Proximity** Stay close as this can bring comfort *(unless the individual has asked to be alone)*.
Safety Minimise the risk of potential harm by removing dangerous items or guiding the person to a safe place.	**Privacy** If possible, redirect bystanders.

Shouting, judgmental stares, pointing, laughing, or negative comments are known to always be unhelpful.

If you aren't sure or worry your action might put you/them at risk - observe and notify a carer or consistent support person to help them.

Regulate, Connect and Support Guide

Supporting Dysregulation

Co-Regulate
This might look like being together but having no pressure to communicate or make eye contact, engaging in interests side-by-side, deep pressure *(e.g. a hug)*, doing heavy work, modelling sensory soothing, engaging with "glimmers" or doing other mindfulness activities.

Recovery
Be sure to wait for signs of recovery as re-escalation *(another meltdown)* is possible if demands, such as communication or activities, are imposed too early.

Remember, if someone loses control, they aren't making a conscious decision about how to behave. They may need to "ride it out" before they can re-regulate.

sunny
spectrum supports

SCAN ME

BIBLIOGRAPHY
In consecutive order

Pg. 7 & 15: Government of South Australia. (2024). *SA Autism Strategy: 2024-2029*. https://inclusive.sa.gov.au/our-work/autismstrategy/sa-first-autism-strategy.

Pg. 9 & 10: Australian Senate. (2022). *Services, support, and life outcomes for Autistic Australians*. https://www.aph.gov.au/Parliamentary_Business/Committees/Senate/Autism/autism/Report.

Pg. 10: Maenner, M. J., Warren, Z., Williams, A. R., Amoakohene, E., Bakian, A. V., Bilder, D. A., Durkin, M. S., Fitzgerald, R. T., Furnier, S. M., Hughes, M. M., Ladd-Acosta, C. M., McArthur, D., Pas, E. T., Salinas, A., Vehorn, A., Williams, S., Esler, A., Grzybowski, A., Hall-Lande, J., . . . Shaw, K. A. (2023). Prevalence and characteristics of autism spectrum disorder among children aged 8 years — Autism and Developmental Disabilities Monitoring Network. *Morbidity and Mortality Weekly Report. Surveillance Summaries*, 72(2), 1–14. https://doi.org/10.15585/mmwr.ss7202a1.

Pg. 13: Skudra, N. (2020). *Chris Packham of Asperger's and Me spent 30 years trying to act normal.* The Art of Autism. https://the-art-of-autism.com/chris-packham-of-aspergers-and-me-spent-30-years-trying-to-act-normal/#:~:text=Furthermore%2C%20Packham's%20perspective%20on%20society's,to%20change%20who%20they%20are.%E2%80%9D.

Pg. 13: Cooper, R., Cooper, K., Russell, A. J., & Smith, L. G. E. (2021). "I'm Proud to be a Little Bit Different": The Effects of Autistic Individuals' Perceptions of Autism and Autism Social Identity on Their Collective Self-esteem. *Journal of Autism and Developmental Disorders*, 51(2), 704–714. https://doi.org/10.1007/s10803-020-04575-4.

Pg. 13: Skudra, N. (2020). Chris Packham of Asperger's and Me spent 30 years trying to act normal. The Art of Autism. https://the-art-of-autism.com/chris-packham-of-aspergers-and-me-spent-30-years-trying-to-act-normal/#:~:text=Furthermore%2C%20Packham's%20perspective%20on%20society's,to%20change%20who%20they%20are.%E2%80%9D.

Pg. 14: American Psychiatric Association. (2022). *Neurodevelopmental Disorders. In Diagnostic and statistical manual of mental disorders* (5, text rev.) https://doi.org/10.1176/appi.books.9780890425787.x01_Neurodevelopmental_Disorders.

Pg. 15 & 16: Autistic Self Advocacy Network. (2021). *Functioning Labels Harm Autistic People*. https://Autisticadvocacy.org/2021/12/functioning-labels-harm-Autistic-people/.

Pg. 16 & 17: Enna Global. (2024). *Why the Autistic Community are Rejecting the Terms "High and Low Functioning"*. https://enna.org/why-the-Autistic-community-are-rejecting-the-terms-high-and-low-functioning/.

Pg. 19-22: Legault, M., Bourdon, JN. & Poirier, P. (2021). From neurodiversity to neurodivergence: the role of epistemic and cognitive marginalization. *Synthese,* 199, 12843–12868. https://doi.org/10.1007/s11229-021-03356-5.

Pg. 22: People with Disability Australia (PWDA). (n.d.). *Models of disability*. https://pwd.org.au/resources/models-of-disability/.

Pg. 24: Hidden Disabilities Sunflower Scheme Limited. (2024). https://hdsunflower.com/au/.

Pg. 28: Kids Helpline. Anxiety in Action: Part 3 - Exploring Fight, Flight, and Freeze Responses (For Kids) [Video]. YouTube. https://www.youtube.com/watch?v=HDFIuNzX19w.

Pg. 28 & 29: Dana, D. (2018). *The Polyvagal theory in therapy. Engaging the rhythm of regulation.* https://psycnet.apa.org/record/2018-26630-000.

Pg. 28 & 29: Porges, S. W. (2022). Polyvagal Theory: A Science of Safety. *Frontiers in Integrative Neuroscience*, 16, 871227–871227. https://doi.org/10.3389/fnint.2022.871227.

Pg. 30 & 31: Siegel, D. (2017). *Dr Dan Siegel's Hand Model of the Brain.* https://drdansiegel.com/hand-model-of-thebrain/.

Pg. 31: Reframing Autism. (n.d.) *Emotional Regulation, Part Two: Using Co-regulation to Teach Emotional Regulation.* https://reframingautism.org.au/emotional-regulation-part-two-using-co-regulation-to-teach-emotional-regulation/.

Pg. 32: Neff, M. A. (2024). *8 Senses of the Body: the Hidden Sensory Systems.* https://neurodivergentinsights.com/blog/8-senses.

Pg. 33: MacLennan, K., O'Brien, S., & Tavassoli, T. (2022). In Our Own Words: The Complex Sensory Experiences of Autistic Adults. *Journal of Autism and Developmental Disorders*, 52(7), 3061–3075. https://doi.org/10.1007/s10803-021-05186-3.

Pg. 34: Cage, E., Di Monaco, J., & Newell, V. (2018). Experiences of autism acceptance and mental health in Autistic adults. *Journal of Autism and Developmental Disorders*, 48(2), 473–484. https://doi.org/10.1007/s10803-017-3342-7.

Pg. 34: Commonwealth of Australia & Education Services Australia. (2024). *Get Ready to Learn: Interoception and self-regulation.* https://studentwellbeinghub.edu.au/educators/topics/interoception-and-self-regulation/.

Pg. 35 & 36: Kapp, S. K., Steward, R., Crane, L., Elliott, D., Elphick, C., Pellicano, E., & Russell, G. (2019). 'People should be allowed to do what they like': Autistic adults' views and experiences of stimming. *Autism: The International Journal of Research and Practice*, 23(7), 1782–1792. https://doi.org/10.1177/1362361319829628.

Pg. 37-40: *The Mighty: 15 People on the Autism Spectrum Describe What a Meltdown Feels Like.*

Pg. 37-40: Reframing Autism. (n.d.). *All about Autistic meltdowns: A guide for allies.* https://reframingautism.org.au/all-about-Autistic-meltdowns-a-guide-for-allies/.

Pg. 37-40: Neurodivergent_Lou. (2023). *Autistic Meltdowns 101*. Facebook. https://www.facebook.com/permalink.phpstory_fbid=pfbid0FukJwQvTaq4j2bn2H48tTvcFHDkdoa2R39w4ACXeJDKfkLgJ4B9JGNEqoUmQnpY1l&id= 100091534964212.

Pg. 37-40: Organization for Autism Research. (2004). The cycle of tantrums, rage, and meltdowns. OARacle Newsletter. https://researchautism.org/oaracle-newsletter/the-cycle-of-tantrums-rage-andmeltdowns/.

Pg. 41 & 42: Reframing Autism. (n.d.). *All about Autistic shutdown: Guide for allies.* https://reframingautism.org.au/all-about-Autistic-shutdown-guide-for-allies/.

Pg. 42: St. Clair, M. C., et al. (2019) *Early risk factors and emotional difficulties in children at risk of Developmental Language Disorder: A Population Cohort Study*

Pg. 42: *Mazurek, M. O., & Kanne, S. M. (2010). Anxiety and comorbid psychiatric disorders in children with autism spectrum disorders. Research in Autism Spectrum Disorders, 4(4), 693-702. DOI: 10.1016/j.rasd.2010.01.012*

Pg. 43: Cai, R. Y., Gibbs, V., Love, A., Robinson, A., Fung, L., & Brown, L. (2023). "Self-compassion changed my life": The self-compassion experiences of Autistic and non-Autistic adults and its relationship with mental health and psychological wellbeing. Journal of Autism and Developmental Disorders, 53(3), 1066–1081. https://doi.org/10.1007/s10803-022-05668-y.

Pg. 44: Mandy, W. (2019). Social camouflaging in autism: Is it time to lose the mask? Autism, 23(8), 1879-1881.

Pg. 46: Arnold, S., Higgins, J., Weise, J., Desai, A., Pellicano, L., & Trollor, J. (2022). Autistic Burnout Final Report. Autism CRC. https://www.autismcrc.com.au/sites/default/files/reports/3-076RI_Autistic-Burnout_Final-report.pdf.

Pg. 48 & 50: MacLennan, Keren & Woolley, Catherine & Emily, & Heasman, Brett & Starns, Jess & George, Becky & Manning, Catherine. (2022). "It Is a Big Spider Web of Things": Sensory Experiences of Autistic Adults in Public Spaces. Autism in Adulthood, 5. https://www.liebertpub.com/doi/10.1089/aut.2022.0024.

Pg. 52: Carol Gray Social Stories. (2024). What is a Social Story?. https://carolgraysocialstories.com/social-stories/what-is-it/.

Pg. 52: Museum of Discovery (MOD.). (2024). Access & Inclusion. https://mod.org.au/visit/access-inclusion/.

Pg. 53: Speech Pathology Australia. (2023). Communication is a human right. https://www.communicationhub.com.au/CommunicationHub/Communication_Hub/Communication_is_a_human_right/Communication_is_essential.aspx.

Pg. 54: Speech Pathology Australia. (2024). Augmentative and Alternative Communication. https://www.speechpathologyaustralia.org.au/Public/Public/Comm-swallow/Aug-alt-strategies/Augmentative-Alternative-Communication.aspx.

Pg. 55 & 56: The Spectrum. (n.d.). Autism communication strategies. https://thespectrum.org.au/autism-strategy/autism-strategy-communication/.

Pg. 55: Lauer, E. (2022). Proper AAC Etiquette: How to Communicate Respectfully with AAC Users. https://spokenaac.com/blog/proper-aac-etiquette/.

Pg. 56: Moore, M. (2022). Autism and Tics: What's the Connection?. https://psychcentral.com/autism/autism-tics#next-steps.

Pg. 56: Rudy, I. J. (2023). Echolalia in Autism: Why Autistic Children Echo Words and Sounds. https://www.verywellhealth.com/why-does-my-child-with-autism-repeat-words-and-phrases-260144.

Pg. 56: Sullivan, D. (2024). Introduction to Echolalia and Autistic Scripting. https://www.neurodiverging.com/introduction-to-echolalia-and-Autistic-scripting/.

Pg. 61 & 62: Capanna-Hodge, R. (2024). Neurotypical vs Neurodivergent Communication: Embracing Diversity in Dialogue. https://drroseann.com/neurotypical-vs-neurodivergent-communication-embracing-diversity-in-dialogue/.

Pg. 62: Amaze. (2017). Information Sheet: How to communicate your message to people on the autism spectrum. https://www.amaze.org.au/wp-content/uploads/2019/06/Amaze-Information-Sheet-How-to-communicate-your-message-to-people-on-the-autism-spectrum.pdf.

Pg. 61 & 62: Milton, D., Gurbuz, E., & López, B. (2022). The 'double empathy problem': Ten years on. Autism, 26(8), 1901-1903. https://doi-org.ezproxy.uow.edu.au/10.1177/13623613221129123.

Pg. 61 & 62: Reframing Autism. (n.d.). Milton's double empathy problem: A summary for non-academics. https://reframingautism.org.au/miltons-double-empathy-problem-a-summary-for-non-academics/

Pg. 62: Crompton, C. J., Ropar, D., Evans-Williams, C. V., Flynn, E. G., & Fletcher-Watson, S. (2020). Autistic peer-to-peer information transfer is highly effective. Autism, 24(7), 1704-1712. https://doi.org/10.1177/1362361320919286.

Pg. 68-71: Autistica. (n.d.). Autism Myths and Causes. https://www.Autistica.org.uk/what-is-autism/autism-myths-and-causes.

Pg. 68-71: Harper, G. (2016). 10 Misconceptions about autism. https://www.ambitiousaboutautism.org.uk/about-us/media-centre/blog/10-misconceptions-about-autism.

Pg. 69: Dresevic, E. (2021). The MMR vaccine does not cause autism. https://www.unicef.org/montenegro/en/stories/mmr-vaccine-does-not-cause-autism.

www.ingramcontent.com/pod-product-compliance
Lightning Source LLC
Chambersburg PA
CBHW061010030426
42334CB00033B/3434